AGENDA

Poetry & Opera

This Poetry & Opera issue of *Agenda* is dedicated to

Seamus Heaney

Above, Eric Banford, Seamus Heaney in St. Lucia with Derek Walcott in 2000

Below, Seamus Heaney and John Robert Lee on a boat

AGENDA

CONTENTS

INTRODUCTION		Patricia McCarthy	8

DEDICATION TO SEAMUS HEANEY: ELEGIES

Derek Walcott:	Heaney in Ireland	10
Greg Delanty:	Goddess of the Hearth	23
	Concealment	23
	The Small Picture	24
	The Blackbird of Lake Champlain	24
John F. Deane:	An Elegy	25
John Robert Lee:	Canticles for Seamus Heaney	26
Eleanor Hooker:	Watermarked	28
Omar Sabbagh:	To The Middle Of Love	29
Sudeep Sen:	Searching for Seamus	30
Patricia McCarthy:	Death of a Bard	31

ESSAYS

William Bedford:	Counting the Syllables: Paul Muldoon as Librettist	33
Neil Powell:	Britten's Books	38
Nigel Jarrett:	Auden, Stravinsky and *The Rake's Progress*	43
Simon Jenner:	Comic Operas and The End of Civilisation	46
Eva Salzman:	Opera More or Less Seria; or an Ensemble of Perplexity	50
Wasfi Kani:	Pimlico Opera is back in prison	60
Karen Anderson	Glyndebourne's outreach work	63

POEMS

David Harsent:	The Salt-Wife	67
Christine McNeill:	Kindertotenlieder	73
	Gustav Mahler on the Rax	83
Jill Townsend	The Auditorium	84
	King Philip's Aria	84
Eleanor Hooker:	Doppelgänger	85
Nancy Anne Miller:	Falling in Love with a Lake	86
John Greening:	All I can remember of Neuschwanstein	87
	Turkish Patrol	87
Andrew McCulloch:	La Scala, 1946	88
	Hopkins' Mother	89
Armand Silvestre:	Two Poems	90
	Translated by Timothy Adès	
Giambattista Marino:	'Battus!' Ergastus Cried	91
	Translated by Timothy Adès	
R.V. Bailey:	Piano	92
Anne Connolly:	Tonic Solfa	93
Sarah Wardle:	Concert for Anarchy	94
	Hope	95
Anne Joyce Mannion:	Turnings	96
Simon Jenner:	Handel in the Arcadian Academy	97
Stuart Medland:	Bert's Avocet	98
	Willow Warbler	99
	Reedling Music	100
Dan MacIsaac:	Northern Shrike	101
	Red Pileated Woodpecker	102
Norman Buller:	Last Songs	103
Warren Stutely:	wight beach winter	104
	beach cubist	105
David Pollard:	Self-Portrait: Maestro Mateo	106
Lawrence Wilson:	modus operandi	108

ESSAYS

David Harsent:	Words for Music	110
Eric Salzman:	Opera, The Writer & The Composer	119
Michael McCarthy:	Poetry and Opera	127
Susan Wicks:	Those Live Moments: Thoughts on Poetry and Music	131
Thomas Adès:	A Path into the Heart – Shakespeare's *The Tempest* translated into opera	134
N. S. Thompson:	Ceyx and Alcyone: Notes for a 'Pocket Opera' in verse	136

POEMS

Sally Long:	When Rebecca Sings	142
James Simpson:	Wind from the North	143
Omar Sabbagh	Breaths Between The Notes	147
	Can I, Daddy: *Can I?*	148
Jonathan Taylor:	Earworm	149
	Numeromania	150
Sally Festing:	On reading *After A Journey*	151
Jim Maguire:	Neurasthenia – Russalka (destroyed), Henri Duparc, 1891	152
Joey Connolly:	Causality	154
Laurelyn Whitt:	Tomboy	155
Jane Clarke:	Dressage	157
Robert Smith:	Die Winterreise	158
	Paul Wittengstein	159
Sebastian Barker	A Treatise on Any Model of Being	160
Martin Bennett:	Starlings	162
Herinder Rai:	The Candle	163
Jay Ramsay:	Requiescat in Pace	164

Tim Murdoch:	Amicitia	166
	Masks	167
Susan Wicks:	United Enemies	168
	Curtains	169
Daniel K. Lee:	In the Dark	170
Jay Rogoff:	All the Same	171
	Travesty	172

BROADSHEET ESSAYIST:

| **Sorana Santos**: | Inextricable Links | 174 |

CHOSEN BROADSHEET POETS:

Benjamin Jack Larner:	Circe	179
	The Shadow Man	182
Sorana Santos:	Bone Ritual	185
	Ocean	187
Kim Moore:	The Musicians	189
	Being a Trumpet Teacher	190
	Ode to my Trumpet	191

NOTES FOR BROADSHEET POETS:

Martin Kratz:	Words and Music, land and sea:	
	On writing a first libretto	193
Sebastian Barker	Judging Poetry	196

Biographies 201

Front cover: Peter Sellar's controversial production of Mozart's *Magic Flute*, set on a Los Angeles freeway by **Carolyn Trant**.

Back cover image by **Carolyn Trant** from Beethoven's *Fidelio* – Glyndebourne 1990 production – the moment when all the prisoners are allowed out of their dungeons for a brief moment of daylight. Etching done from drawings made at rehearsals at the invitation of Glyndebourne.

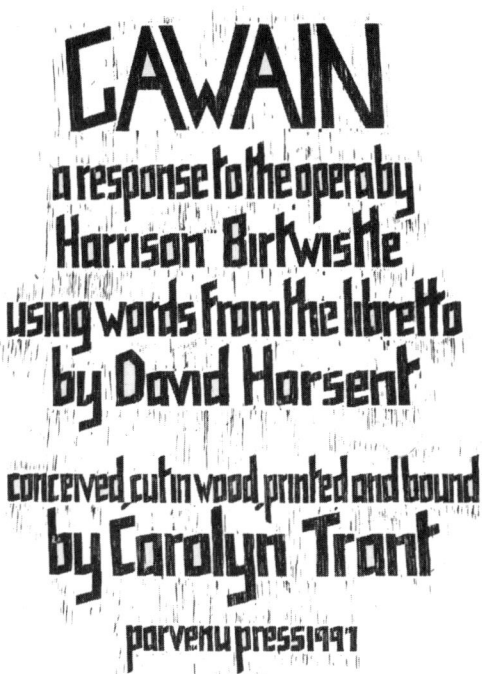

Carolyn Trant, formerly a painter, has been making Artists Books and woodcut prints for about twenty years. One of the very first was 'Gawain', a response to David Harsent's libretto for Harrison Birtwistle's opera of the same name, images from which are used throughout this Poetry & Opera issue.

She has always had a passion for opera and in 1990 was invited to work at Glyndebourne for a season making images of the gardens and rehearsals. Making scribble images in the dark of swiftly moving actions and trying to capture the emotions in the gestures was more exciting than 'life drawing'. These scribbles were transferred to the soft ground of the etching plate. Using aquatint and intaglio combined with relief printing an attempt was made to reproduce the rich colours of the lit stage.

Making Artists Books with images, and texts often written by other people, is in some ways like an opera director interpreting a musical piece. The artist is choreographing the movement of the pages; the binding, proportions and margins are a stage set for the images and words and determine pace and rhythm. The re-interpretation of meaning from text to image is akin to the transformation that takes place in each conductor and musician's new performance of a musical piece.

Carolyn has also made other books inspired by music – for example Schubert's Winterreise; and worked with several other contemporary poets.

Her work is in many private and public collections across the UK (British Library, Tate, V&A) USA, Europe and Australia. www.carolyntrant.co.uk

Introduction

It was with great sadness and shock that we heard of the sudden death of Seamus Heaney, a great friend, and wonderful supporter of *Agenda*. We pay tribute to him in the first section of this issue, including a very special essay on Heaney and Ireland by his fellow Nobel Laureate poet and friend, Derek Walcott. It must be quite unique to have one Nobel Laureate poet writing on another.

Seamus Heaney, to whom this special double Poetry & Opera issue is dedicated, should have, therefore, I think, the first word in the lively debate about what he calls 'the ancient lyric discipline of fitting words to music' between librettists/poets and composers. He refers to 'the trading of rhymes and syllables, the give of speech and the take of song' in his setting of words to music for Janáček's song cycle, *Diary of One who Vanished*, first performed in 1999 by the English National Opera. To him, the making of 'a new singable translation' of poems originally printed in a local Moravian newspaper (later identified to be the work of Ozef Kalda) was 'an excitement and an education'.

This issue also celebrates the centenary of Benjamin Britten, born November 22, 1913, on, by a happy coincidence, St. Cecilia's Day, the latter being the patroness of music. A recent publication of a substantial tome, *Benjamin Britten: A Life for Music* (Hutchinson, 2013) by Neil Powell, who has an enlightening essay here on Britten's books, is well worth a read. A good handbook, hot off Carcanet Press, to Powell's book is *Benjamin Britten's Poets*, edited by Boris Ford: an anthology of poems that Britten set to music.

It is evident from the ensuing pages that opera has an important future, not just as an élitist art form for the wealthy, but as an educational, vibrant, inventive life force that cuts across social and cultural boundaries. Composer Eric Salzman and his poet daughter Eva Salzman especially attest to this, as do Michael McCarthy from Mid Wales Opera, Glyndebourne's vast outreach work, and Wasfi Kanu of Grange Park Opera whose branch of this, Pimlico Opera, does therapeutic, educational and grounding work with prisoners, helping them to adjust to ordinary life after release.

I myself studied Music at Trinity College Dublin, under Professor Brian Boydell, an inspiring man and a considerable composer well established in Ireland. To this day I have orange spiral-bound exercise books that – in my neater handwriting – copied down what he so interestingly said as we covered The History of Music, including, of course, opera. I do recall writing a long essay on Gluck's reform of eighteenth century opera, how, as J.A. Hiller said, 'Gluck has made a music that is his own; or rather he has sought in nature all the sounds of true expression and conquered them for himself.' He apparently learned to make his lines straightforward by attending David Garrick's performances of Shakespeare in London. He liked that natural way of acting. It is interesting to note how his influence is still felt today! I recall, too, the influence on opera of the lied or solo song which suggests the idea of music which actually illustrates words, accompanied by the rise of the piano as a sensitive enough instrument to harmonise the modulations and literal meanings in the voice. The major achievement here was the subtle wedding of poetry and music, the ideal duet between piano and voice: what the best in opera strives for and achieves, surely, on a larger scale. Schubert in particular springs to mind, with his special insight into poetry, and ability to penetrate into the central meaning of the poem. Hugo Wolf, too, I remember studying, whose greatest musical insights centred on the poems of Morike. He probed the heart of the poem for its meaning even more profoundly than Schubert. His tragic life ended in an asylum in 1903, perhaps not the best model for today's librettists!

Interestingly, W S Milne has pointed out how Stravinsky decided to call his series of lectures on Composition (delivered at Harvard) *The Poetics of Music* – the poet and the composer making order out of chaos.

Let us see, then, what we make, in the ensuing pages, of the complex collaboration between composer and librettist, of 'the give of speech and the take of song.'

Patricia McCarthy

SUBSCRIBE SUBSCRIBE SUBSCRIBE SUBSCRIBE SUBSCRIBE SUBSCRIBE

Future issues of *Agenda*:

Spring 2014: double Anthology issue: poems, essays, reviews
Autumn/Winter 2014: Special double issue on World War I including a section on Edward Thomas.

Submissions
For Spring 2014 issue: no particular theme.
For Autumn/Winter 2014 issue: poems inspired by original familial/ancestral, researched, historical experiences in The Great War.

SUBSCRIBE SUBSCRIBE SUBSCRIBE SUBSCRIBE SUBSCRIBE SUBSCRIBE

Derek Walcott

Heaney in Ireland

i

Away to the house of death.
To my father, sitting waiting there
Under the clay roof. I'll come back to him
Out of the light, out of his memory
Of the day I left.
        ('The Cure at Troy')

The new grave was glowing with fresh wreaths and the cards on the wreaths were still unstained, not streaked by any drizzle. There were two or three other graves, Devlins all around. A high old cross and, against clouds, a theatrically barren tree. What I thought was the sea down the slope with a large rut in it was really the lake. Black and white cattle moved and occasionally lowed quietly as they moved. There was a headstone. There was stillness, except for the cows, with no sound from the water, no birds or anything crying. In the chill but bracing air in a raincoat in an old cemetery, it was like a film, with a film's carefulness about location. Two men with springy leashed greyhounds followed them along the path through the graves.

   In a light drizzle we drove back to the house to meet Marie Heaney (née Devlin), and Marie had to leave the house and, down the road from the house, the new grave above the old lake, where the Devlins lie. It was like unnecessary Chekhov, leaving the empty house. A car drew up behind us when we stopped. It was Seamus's brother, Hugh.

   Seamus signed new copies of the limited edition for Hugh on top of Hugh's car, while I walked to the edge of the banked road and looked over the hedge, where I saw the field; so nature acquires the accent of the language in which a good poet describes it, and Hugh's heavy Derry accent became part of the shrub and the tree. This happens with the light, the weather which a poet gets correctly. Anahorish.

   The peace of Ireland was passing by on the drive, and what was centrally contained in Seamus's poetry was also passing through, and permanent, the window glass. The tight coil of his lines, on which the words cluster like berries eaten one at a time, and along which there is a close-leafed thickening that, stripped like a rod, would still show a live and plant branch, the small walled fields, the morning rain on the grey lake, the tight cottages, and the old trees of the dipping road to Derry were confirming the verse. The verse and the voice itself.

A true voice, rooted in its compact geography, its exact region, takes its accent from that geography, but also returns it. The 'local habitation and a name' of Shakespeare is exactly the 'local', so that the places mutely sounded like their names in the verse: Armagh, Anahorish, Donegal, muttering their names in their regional accents, in Heaney's written and actual voice:

> My 'place of clear water'
> the first hill on the world
> where spring's washed into
> the shiny grass
> and darkened cobbles
> on the bed of the lane.
> Anahorish, soft gradient
> of consonant, vowel-meadow

or through passages of enclosing lanes, because concealment was strategy, and because the psychology of terror lay not in alarms or warnings, not in orderly assault, but in shock and surprise, in the tension of the normal, when the ticking of an old-fashioned bomb was the same sound as that of a clock on the mantel. And that is how they must live their normal lives in the North, in the city of Belfast, waiting for the clock on the mantel to go off with the bomb on the head, the wrist, the heart.

> Hide in the hollow trunk
> of the willow tree,
> its listening familiar,
> until, as usual, they
> cuckoo your name
> across the fields.
> You can hear them draw the poles of stiles
> as they approach calling you out:
> small mouth and ear
> in a woody cleft,
> lobe and larynx
> of the mossy places.
> ('Orack')

In Derry, in the North, it was a mild and bright October, September finishing, and in the old walled city Heaney's first play had just opened.

Called *The Cure at Troy*, it was his translation, via cribs, of Sophocles' story about another outcast, another figure thrown out of society and the warmth of companionship, Philoctetes. Seamus refers to the play, his version, as 'homework', an assignment given to him by The Field Day Theatre Company.

The designer, Bob Crowley, reduced the play's setting, on the island of Lemnos, with the simplicity of genius: a hollow white rectangle draped in cloth, which, as the crinkling material, like a fog at sea, lifted, revealed a chorus of three women in robes the colour of rusted blood, stone-still, and, in one corner of the marble-white box, the huge cracked head of a fallen god. Except for the figure of Philoctetes, this crusted red, like splotches against marble, unified the metaphors of the wound, while Philoctetes, when he appeared, seemed to emerge from a cave that was the hollow of the fallen god's head, ragged and bandaged, and dusted with marble, like a man on the way to becoming a statue himself, or a resurrected corpse.

It was an excellent, fine-spoken Chorus, with a clear, perhaps too clear, and not duplicitous enough Odysseus played by Sean Moran, and a somewhat jejune Neptolemus played by Sean Rocks. The burden of the acting was carried by Des McAleer as Philoctetes, who wonderfully alternated his pitches from a gruff, conversational bittterness to a deep resonant bellow that soared to a curdling scream. The Derry Guildhall was not the best place for the setting, and it took some time to settle into the mood of the play, but the play would be touring Ireland, and the set was designed for easy dismantling and mounting. The direction looked too stately, as if it were too in awe of the event, and of the language, Sophocles via Heaney. It lacked fury of movement, a horror of vertigo.

This was Field Day's tenth year, as long as the siege of Troy. But the siege ended in Troy, while the wound of Northern Ireland had no set date, no curtain, no lights fading and rising to applause, no god descending from the machine as Hercules does in the original, to resolve and cure. In a sense Heaney had no choice but to remove the god from his text. Hercules does not appear. The wound remains open. No civic catharsis is offered. In the way that prisoners grow fond of their cells, the wounded can nurture their sores, is what Heaney's moral seems to be. That Ireland, bitterly enough, may enjoy being Ireland, torn, divided, bleeding in its isolation, because, according to the Irish, that is the nature of the beast. The cure, the play harshly admonishes its countrymen, is within.

CHORUS:
Your wound is what you feed on, Philoctetes.
I say it again in friendship and say this:
Stop eating yourself up with hate and come with us.

The Cure at Troy, with its central figure of an abandoned warrior, Philoctetes, hobbling around a barren island where he has been left by his shipmates because of a foul-smelling, incurable wound, is an immediate symbol of Ireland's own affliction. It occasioned embittered puns from Seamus's Field Day colleagues, one of them being the connection of ulcer with Ulster. Because Philoctetes also figures in a work of mine, I said to Seamus, 'suppuration is in,' and he winced at my crassness. There were worse puns, though, twice as horrific.

Some critics wanted more parallels from the text, and Heaney had included contemporary references to Belfast, but they were kept spare, and in fact spareness, fidelity to the text, provided a judging distance, since propaganda was easy, and moral outrage threatened to make Sophocles provincial and his play adapted and exploited for various reasons.

I wanted more of Sweeney in the text myself. But the adaptation is humble, even chaste, and when I heard and read it later, Heaney's intention was clear: to write clearly, to give the speeches and exchanges the same frosty glitter of a northern spring, a translucency rather than a translation, of moving the original setting too obviously, too accommodatingly to Northern Ireland. But I still felt cheated of a little more wildness in the text, more natural and also inner rough weather, more gusts and flashes than are now in the decent, nearly reticent simplicity of the language. Heaney must have felt that he did not want the shadow of style to fall across the light of Sophocles' language, which in the case of the original *Lir* (later *King Lear*), had Shakespeare stuck to such modesty, would have deprived us of glory. But the power of Sophocles, the simplicity of an aged mind, must lie in the fierceness of clarity, like a steady consuming light, and although the text of *The Cure of Troy* has a cautious power, closer to, say, the diction of W.C. Williams than to the rough nap of a contemporary like Ted Hughes, the ease of its scansion and the determined invisibility of Heaney is laudable, and its lift subtly Irish.

> CHORUS:
> It's a pity of him too
> Afflicted like that.
> Him and that terrible foot.

At breakfast, windows overlooking the estuary, bright sunlight on the hammered water, the headland beginning to show its greens and blue-greys, soft relentless musak poured over the sunlit tables, one of the tunes, 'When I Grow Too Old To Dream', a favourite of my mother's, and the melody, moving with the moving water soundless through the plate glass, had the auld Irish melancholy, a country that could move from violence to sweetness, harps and flutes, where every provisional could be an unfulfilled tenor. In the music there was the thought of Marie's father's death, and the wreaths I had seen yesterday, and those from my mother's funeral some months before.

In the play there were painful passages that dealt with the deaths of fathers. The death of Achilles was news brought to the ulcerous Philoctetes by Achilles' son. They must have been hard to bear.

> PHILOCTETES:
> Away to the house of death.
> To my father, sitting waiting there
> Under the clay roof. I'll come back to him
> Out of the light, out of his memory
> Of the day that I left.

Marie and Seamus liked to sing together. Marie had a fine voice. They sang after dinner at Cambridge parties. The music moved from 'Streets of Laredo' to 'Bendermeer's Stream' with lines I used to sing to myself as well as I could, and still like: 'And say, is the nightingale singing there yet?' So I surrendered, gave up this typing and leant back to let the tears do what they had to. Two countries I know have this continual melody, Trinidad and Ireland. Both sprout bards like bush. My mother. All those songs, where did she get them? 'Smiling Through', 'It's a Long Way To Tipperary', 'Danny Boy', 'Mother Machree', 'Danny Boy' was 'Londonderry Air'. (You said London if you were from Ulster and Derry alone if you were Republican). Tipperary lay ahead, and other places with tunes either martial or nostalgic. The intimacies cannot be separated from what lies ahead this morning: a ride down to Dublin, through counties after which melodies were named.

Then, near the bridge out of Derry, we saw soldiers, two armoured lorries curving around, and fresh pink faces above the camouflage uniforms, containing the history of siege and defence of the old walled city, a sight familiar to Seamus but to me, shocking. As shocking as the white gendarmes with their kepis and shorts that one sees in the French departments of Martinique and St. Martin, a swift sensation of nausea that took some time to pass.

'Ah, they're all right,' Seamus said. They looked like boys, but soldiers everywhere were boys. The grumble was surly but also paternal. They were lads, and he had two admirable sons their age, Michael and Christopher, who themselves could have been at risk, on whichever side, in whatever lorries. And the bright faces muted the anonymity of their uniforms for a moment. This was the child sensation, like a chill drizzle along the nerves of:

So you drive on to the frontier of writing
where it happens again. The guns on tripods:
the sergeant with his on-off mike repeating

data about you, waiting for the squawk
of clearance; the marksman training down
out of the sun upon you like a hawk.

The best Irish poets today come from the North: Derek Mahon, Tom Paulin, John Montague, Paul Muldoon, Michael Longley, and Heaney. I had thought of their work collectively, in terms of barren wet streets, not of pastoral. All of them have moved away. There are devouring pettinesses in Ireland, bigotry, provincialism that drove others away: Beckett, Joyce, that enraged O'Casey and Patrick Kavanagh, who saw its worst aspects as those of a stubborn, lumpy society, priest-ridden and hypocritical, garrulous and drunken, too witty for its own good. Joyce had called it 'the sow that eats its farrow', its art 'the cracked looking glass of a servant'. Swift and even Yeats had raged at it, calling it a place of 'great hatred, little room'. Heaney's Sweeney sings:

You are welcome to pledge healths
and carouse in your drinking dens:
I will dip and steal water
from a well with my open balm.

You are welcome to that cloistered hush
of your students' conversation;
I will study the pure chant
Of hounds baying in Glen Bolcain.

On an earlier trip, in Dublin, I had imagined the North, because of all the propaganda surrounding it on all sides, as a barren and desolate place, without the emerald, wet lushness of the southern counties; but the narrow, leafy and dipping road out of Derry, in the early fall, was as fresh as a watercolour, with hints of orange bushes and trees, and sudden surprising meadows, some with sheep or horses or cattle. I had asked Seamus if the North was as beautiful as the South, and I believe he said, 'Better,' with the old provincial patriotism, and it was as good. To me, they were all the same, and I lost my sense of boundary and division, of shadow and strife, in the wonderful light.

There seemed to be no noon in Ireland. The light simply slanted in long, cool shadows from right to left, or east to west, as though the dial had glided from ten in the morning to late afternoon. No stasis, no stunning heat. There were high, creamy clouds that the light broke through, making patterns on the low hills with windbreaks. Orange and green was North and South, the fall itself political, cohering the conflicting colours of Orangeman and Republican. Would these natural colours always return as inevitably as the colours of civil conflict? It is an island without too many freeways. Roads follow their contours.

The green of Ireland was proverbial, but so was its lyrical vehemence, its emblems, like 'The Wearing of the Green', a marching song.

Streets and countryside were benign. But in the car we were soon talking about the violence of ambush while the serene landscapes rolled past the panes that was the pain of Ireland, I guessed, the beauty that in Yeats' easy phrase became terrible. The sound 'Belfast', like 'Beirut' had terror in it. The terror. Terrorism. In this time terrorism and patriotism interchange, depending on where you stand. The only wars possible as technology becomes monolithic may be guerrilla wars, and guerrilla wars do not have, like our idea of military battles, our acceptance of neat, uniformed casualties.

Dublin has no skyline, no high-rises. The long, long curve of bay still has been spared those blocks that now make every city in America synonymous. The provinciality in Ireland is its strength, in architecture as well as in its poetry.

Very pleasant, the high wide room of the hotel, with windows in every wall, overlooking the sweep of Howth, the bay with its ferry and, on brighter mornings, sailboats, with Joyce's Martello Tower just down the road, and autumn edging more colour into the trees. Very large the Irish breakfasts, with great bread, kippers and tea. The light on the walls like butter. Dublin is a pleasant, ambling place, small and with that urgent provinciality that small cities have, that neighbourliness is possible, hard to imagine any hatred beneath it, or to justify, in the benign sunlight, the implacable, stony bitterness of Belfast.

So this was an Irish cottage, in Ireland, not a Georgian retreat in England, and although many of the lines sway gently to the metre of similar branches from Edward Thomas, 'And elderberry I have learned to call it,' in that very vicinity the pastoral can cloud, darken, the branches bleed, the sap drips poison, and we can turn into a wood whose meter becomes hair-raising, like Macbeth's:

Thunderlight on the split logs; big raindrops
At body heat and lush with omen
Spattering dark on the hatchet iron.
This morning when a magpie with jerky steps

> Inspected a horse asleep beside the wood
> I thought of dew on armour and carrion.
> What would I meet blood-boltered, on the road?
> How deep into the woodpile sat the toad?

The island, the cottage, the cell, the hermitage is as endangered, as torn by violent memory of artillery, of butchery, of huge tears, of crows pecking dead horses in a battlefield as any street in Belfast.

The Heaneys' house is close to the bay, its front bright with some kind of ivy, its living room deep and used, very familial. There are three children: two sons as I have already mentioned, and a daughter, Catherine, who has that cold, rosy skin of black-haired Irish beauties. About forty minutes away from Dublin, the Heaneys have a cottage in Glanmore, the gatehouse of an estate, with no telephone, where they lived for some time before moving to Dublin. This is the cottage of the Glanmore sonnets. Over a low hedge beyond the cottage is a wide, rolling field. The road alongside it was small and leafy with, what to my eyes, were huge roses near the walls.

The Heaneys had lived in Glanmore for years, and he celebrates that period in 'Glanmore Sonnets'. This piece would be a violation of their intimacy, Seamus's and Marie's, if that intimacy had not been opened gently, by Seamus himself, like a creaking page:

> This evening the cuckoo and the corncrake
> (So much, too much) consorted at twilight.
> It was all crepuscular and iambic.
> Out on the field a baby rabbit
> Took his bearings, and I knew the deer
> (I've seen them too from the window of the house,
> Like connoisseurs, inquisitive of air)
> Were careful under larch and May-green spruce.
> I had said earlier, 'I won't relapse
> From this strange loveliness I've brought us to.
> 'Dorothy and William.' She interrupts:
> 'You're not going to compare us two?' ...
> Outside a rustling and twig-combing breeze
> Refreshes and relents. Is cadences.

ii

Bricks of peat were smoking in the cottage hearth. The peat had a pleasing smell and was not what I had imagined it to be before my first visit to Ireland.

The bricks were dug and cut from bogs and stacked in a pattern in which their blocks supported one another in an ancient design, some kind of Celtic geometry that went way back. Then, on the first visit, Seamus had shown us a field with the brownish-black turf open and a sliced scarp that was the bog. Before, the word had had a feel of foundering, of muck and squelch, edged with fear, of the horror of sinking up to the neck in mud, like some passage in Dante and Conan Doyle. Perhaps the rhyme with fog had created this, an aural as well as a visual echo. These echoes, made by imagination and not experience, by association instead of sight, are hard to shed beyond boyhood when thousands of miles away, on an island on the other side of the world, where there is no fog, only mist, no seasons changing, no hearths and no peat. I'd shuddered at the word. Fog meant the Hound of the Baskervilles loping outside our house; bog meant ogres and dripping, clawing branches. But in the cottage at the hearth of their rhymer, the bog bricks smelt sweet, and the bog itself, around the dug earth, with all its weedy paths and grass and unknown flowers, was as lovely as the hearth scent, a place from a hardworking childhood that Seamus the boy cherished and Heaney the bog-poet celebrates. Joyce has a lovely pun in *Finnegan's Wake*: 'the oak trees peats be with them', and, oh, another: 'that forestfellfoss', and in the peat-scented (unless memory has sweetened it) smell of the small parlour in Glanmore, Seamus looked ample and content, and the talk among the four of us, Marie, Sigrid, Seamus, and me, was easy and rich.

Poets guard and cherish, if they are that blessed, some place of seclusion. In bog and fire and cottage Heaney was glowing in his element. Marie was as much that element as the bright trees outside and the cool field over the hedges, and the hollow base of a riven oak from which weeds grew in its wooden basin.

So what did we talk about? Answering that question in one of the Cantos, Pound wrote: '*de litteris at de armis*', 'of books and armies', but behind the chat there was a deeper pleasure than affability, a rooting, also there in Pound's 'Is that not our delight / to have friends come from far countries?' Both quotations sounded as if they were from Horace. There is a merriment in Seamus's company, which comes from his delight in his occupation. But it seems to me that all good poets, away from their work, which is language, share a light-headedness, an enjoyment of puns which is a kind of self-mockery, an undermining of solemnity. The glitter and light of his northern fields made his pleasure unforced, infectious and natural. The man showing you his boy's life was more boy than man. Like Billy Wordsworth. Grasmere is Wordsworth's cottage, Glanmore is Heaney's.

    Soft corrugations in the boortree's trunk,
    Its green young shoots, its rods like freckled solder:

> It was our bower as children, a greenish, dank
> And snapping memory as I get older.
> And elderberry ...

Nice pun there: 'elderberry' as he gets older ...

> And elderberry I have learned to call it.
> I love its blooms like saucers brimmed with meal,
> Its berries a swart caviar of shot,
> A buoyant spawn, a light bruised out of purple.
> Elderberry? It is shires dreaming wine.
> Boortree is bower tree, where I played 'touching tongues'
> And felt another's texture quick on mine.
> So, etymologist of roots and graftings,
> I fall back to my tree-house and would crouch
> Where small buds shoot and flourish in the hush.

We were talking about Seamus's beginnings as a poet. He had been published almost immediately by Faber, and one early review had referred to his first book, its bog and peat origins, its digging for those blocks in the hearth, as 'mud-caked fingers in Russell Square'. I reminded him of how, after reading a review that, in rough memory, referred to him as the blue-eyed boy of English poetry, implying that there is always a poet who becomes fashionable and sells well for other reasons than his verse, I had sent him a note cursing the reviewer. It was hard to know what critics wanted from poetry. Dignity was in poor sales, popularity was a Judas kiss, while they advanced the cause in prose and complained about obscurity and neglect. Critics always imply that they would have defended Keats from their own kind or that they would have collected Van Goghs. A friendship had come about through that abuse, though.

The two roads that diverged for the young Heaney: Yeats or Kavanagh.

Kavanagh's subjects found their relaxed metres easily, because their tone was laid-back, the mutterings and abrasions of a voice supported by a pint in a pub booth, moving in their natural pitch from a surly bass growl to a tenor sentimentality, happy to settle in and, out of that cantankerous confidence, to reinforce the cliché of the poet as pub-prophet, sudden singer, companion of tinkers, blind to everything else but his holy vocation. 'I am Raftery, the poet.' Kavanagh won his voice by listening to it. This is rarer than supposed. To deafen oneself to the urgencies of modern poetry, which quickly became the property of academics and reviewers, he needed to besiege himself, to armour his tenderness with professional irascibility, an unflinching carapace of playing the outcast, but in a gregarious vocabulary. He made the pub his island, and the noises within that island entered his hearing, just as the liquid yet rocky sea-sway and crash entered Synge's ear on the Aran Islands. Helicon was a public canal. The glittering surface of the canal, the little corrugations of the 'm's as if in the wake of a barge, but most of all the exact, provincial audacity of the word 'water' being pronounced in the one and only way, Irishly, the ancient bravery of beginning with an invocation in which the word 'O' is like the mouth of a sluice from which the line corrugates liquidly, remains private, a different 'O' from Yeats's. A man praising in comfort on a bench, not striding on a tower's parapet. Yeats stands up. Kavanagh sits down:

O commemorate me where there's water.

Then the startling:

Niagarously roars,

which is epical, Miltonic, yet exquisitely private, an echo in the inner ear, still not the public address, not theatrical.

This muting, these snarled asides, contemptuous of praise but dreading it, and this deliberate falling off the Yeats bicycle, like a man trying to ride or write all over, this calculated awkwardness that made Hardy more modern than his successors, how to incorporate hesitancy, search, and bathos into music, the disjunctive rather than the harmonious, this more deeply domesticated Irishness, for all its risk of cliché and given emblem, tinker, farmer, priest, bicycle, hedges, rain, potatoes, birds, and bogs, held on to by Kavanagh, gave the early Heaney example and solidity. But Kavanagh's mastery lay in the aside, the slur, or in unabashed open singing, the 'O's of an amateur tenor at the piano hitting the auld favourites, and the embarking Heaney knew that only wisdom, or at least experience, entitles a young maker to the aside; only a bitter confidence like Kavanagh's earned the right to satire and the slurred phrase, and it is remarkable in Heaney that he obeyed the disciplines of his vocation so tenaciously, that, untouched by Eliot or Pound, like some farmer's lad who had never heard of the modern (this is a cunning that has turned into authority), he fought off Yeats and, remarkably, Auden too, but he also did not succumb to slackness, to a loose gargling of Oirish, as Kavanagh's disciples did, because the young Heaney wanted to sing, a muted song of course, stanzaically tense, yet with its core quiet.

Quiet is an attribute of agricultural poetry, wide fields in lines, pre-dawn dark, bird-alphabets at dusk, and the stolid silence of farm stock. So that the creak of a pump, the clang of a bucket had to be caught without spilling over into the next line's caesura. The lines are like rims, of bucket or trough; they should contain and not spill, leak, or drain. But the inevitable threat lay in music, in the popular ballad. Heaney wants to write ballads because it is a tradition, no, an occupation as hereditary as farming, but he wants to write tough ones, coarse-textured, as privately colloquial as Kavanagh's. For poets, once the landscape has passed from exhilaration to habit, another language is always needed. Heaney is coring his vocabulary towards an interior silence, not in flight from political faction, not islanding himself in conspicuous hermitage, but rather as a pilgrim towards a stiller centre, an inward murmur, a hum, not a hymn. This is the map of 'Station Island'. Only: the liturgical word 'Retreat', for Heaney, is not withdrawal into contemplation among other pilgrims but the process of examination, the question of what vocabulary to worship in, with what nouns, what stones to pile a private, primal cairn as the foundations of awe. The climate around him is one of fear, but we cannot live without fear, otherwise faith is unnecessary. That is its irony. And, under Dante, the shadowy guide of the pilgrimage in 'Station Island', Heaney, in the Ghibelline-Guelph civil strife updated by Catholic and Protestant, by North and South, has experienced the irony of a violence based on faith. Here are two different speakers from his *Purgatorio*:

> If times were hard, I could be hard too.
> I made the traitor in me sink the knife.
> And maybe there's a lesson there for you.

and

> I turned to meet his face and the shock
>
> is still in me at what I saw. His brow
> was blown open above the eye and blood
> had dried on his neck and cheek. 'Easy now,'
> he said, 'it's only me. You've seen men as raw
> after a football match ...

Purgatorio is the most theatrical of the *Comedy*'s triptych, because it is winged on either side, like a medieval stage platform, by a painted heaven and a painted hell, dogmatically emblematic, and it is the middle of both visions on either wing that the dilemma, ambiguity, temptation, and irony of human middleness asserts and contradicts itself. *Purgatorio* is the book of doubt. Hell and Heaven are certain. For a poet in a civil war every utterance in that middle position will contain those ironies and ambiguities, and every poem will seem theatrical. Yeats presumed this and worked out a rhetoric that was factional by being patriotic, despite his famous

> Hurrah for revolution and more cannon-shot!
> A beggar upon horseback lashes a beggar on foot.

in which the roles are cyclically, cynically reversed.

But Yeats' day is not Heaney's, it is not the time of O'Casey and Synge, it is not even Kavanagh's day, and just as the revolution of one epoch or decade does not work for another time, so, because the temperature of the facts change, whatever the audacity of the passion, neither does the rhetoric of one epoch work for a later one. We wish that Ben Jonson had written more intimately about Shakespeare, because behind the pretext of criticism, even of awe, there is what is more interesting than literature: life. Better plotted, always symmetrical, with its unvariable beginning, middle and end, and for that reason gossip is more interesting than criticism. What was Tolstoy like on Monday morning, laundry day; what did Chekhov talk about at dusk; and did Shakespeare have big feet is really, without kidding ourselves, at least as important as their work. Instead, we go through this ritual of distancing, of neutralising friendship for the sake of art. But one of the things about rites is the observation of them and I suppose I have to observe rules and subjugate my friendship with Seamus, Seamus Heaney – that genial, generous man with stilted merriment in his eyes – to that other, the reader, who is supposed to know him through his work, that 'pure chant'.

Greg Delanty

For Heanius – Seamus Heaney

Goddess of the Hearth

And what about Hestia? We know little of her story.
      Where's the record of Penelope
and Telemachus playing checkers before the fire?
      Or the version in which Odysseus escaped the draft,
never left for Troy, enjoyed the solace
      of arriving home after work, pouring a glass of wine,
playing with his boy, having given thanks to the goddess?
      Hestia, as unassuming as many wives, husbands,
parents slaving at chores without a word
      of thanks, feeding the hearth, the embers rekindled.

Concealment

A man walked past. We practically
      brushed shoulders, the lane was so narrow.
I nodded, muttered a *kalimera*, but
      he chose to look ahead, ignore me.
I've seen that look, that demeanor before,
      always in rural towns, villages:
Toome, Morrisville, Derrynane, Delphi.
      Not simply the buttoned-up look that is the result
of living in a small community,
      but the face that stubbornly shuts out the invasion
of sightseers, yuppy realtors, outsiders.
      It conceals the gold bar of butter,
rancid or no, left buried in the bog,
      safe from any museum,
the last salted treasure of the lost world.

The Small Picture

to Heanius and Christopher Silentiarius

The priest rambles on about how we're each a particle of sand,
    – such a tiresome analogy – that everyone should take a grain,
consider it in the light between thumb and index finger
    not unlike the position I hold my pen now.
I almost spoke up, said he's making too much of us,
    that this grain of sand is more like our star, our sun.
Imagine then a speck too small for the eye to see, our earth.
    Then imagine ourselves in the big picture. Yes,
I know my place, but today your few words of praise
    – what does it matter what you praised? –
made me forget my smallness. Puffed me up.
    Comedic as it sounds. Who knows,
it may be true. Who knows, we all may be worthwhile. Imagine.

The Blackbird of Lake Champlain

On hearing Seamus Heaney has died

> *The small bird*
> *Chirp-chirruped:*
> *Yellow neb,*
>   *A note-spurt.*
>
> from 'The Blackbird of Belfast Lough',
> Translated from the Irish by Seamus Heaney

The redwing blackbird is perched on electric wires,
    a note on a score, the red epaulets
tipped with deckled gorse-gold. How far
    he's come. How far he has to go.
        How lonely the sound.

Note: The Blackbird is a symbol of poetry in the Irish tradition

John F. Deane

An Elegy

Flora in the roadside ditch
are boasting the water-colour purple of a pride of bishops –
vetch, knapweed, clover and the rosebay willow herb;
and I would make a poem

the way old Brückner caught a flight of pelicans in his
Ecce sacerdos magnus...
for eight-part choir, key magenta, though these times the spirit
slumps, mal-tended in this limping country. Now

a blackcap, fast and furtive, comes to feast on the white berries
of the dogwood hedge; a bullfinch,
secretive, subdued, flits in a shock of rose-petal black and white
across the alder thicket

and I am urged to praise, willing to have the poem
speak the improbable wonderful. Today
the poet Seamus Heaney said he was leaving us for a while,
visiting high mountain pastures,

and seeing things.
I have been walking, grieved, the Slievemore heathlands
and watching a sheep-dog,
low-crouched, eager, waiting for the sheepman's whistle;

furze blazed with a cool gold flame; the sheep
were marked with blobs of red and purple dye, cumbered
with dried-in mud; while out on the bay
the Crested Grebe moved, masterful, in brown Connemara tweed.

John Robert Lee

Canticles for Seamus Heaney 1939-2013

i

On the radio, classical music from horizon-clear Martinique.

Mid-October, mid-afternoon, light breezes under the over-spreading mango,
across envined palmiste, through the abandoned garden, and you imagine
the shadows
lacquered, set. The antique
stone staircase reduced to one forlorn curve and a few broken flagstones
leans against the shade. In the frame, between grasses, is that an egret?
Pastoral pauses at Mount Pleasant, above Castries, in sight of Morne du
Don villas,
                              high palms edging
the drift of hill across its barricade

of blue bent space.
                Seamus Heaney,
phone calls from Stockholm, the graduation of apprentices,
afternoon softening to pastel, numinous,
over Choc's procession of bright stones – what urgent
apocalypse hesitates to interrupt the coralita flirting among golden crotons?

On the radio, creole music of Malavoi from Martinique.

ii

"Places of writing" – Sandymount Strand to Becune Point
by way of Mossbawn and Chaussée Road
then to Choc and Bellaghy – our corners and yours

where hens squawk under guava trees
and I imagine furrows of Derry in Autumn mists
the blackbird frantic on the skylight of Glanmore –

and Creole violons you loved with their ancient men
are gathering on Walcott's surf-splattered verandah
with remembrances of you in *lakonmet* and *moolala*

and always, always, joynoise of friends and shac-shac players
tuned with our poteen. Ah Seamus!
We strike our notes and dig to roots of ploughs.

iii

'Noli timere,' fear not, as we open the roof of clods
and let him down the mosswalls of Bellaghy
among the scattered cloths and beds

of poets, prophets and men of the palsy
who fall to Compassion in the hammocks of Love
and rise and walk in the grace of Mercy

gratefully.
                      Harmonies of harps and violons lift above
Carrauntoohil and Morne Gimie, Castle Dawson and Castries.

Eleanor Hooker

Watermarked

i.m Seamus Heaney

At thirteen, my chosen poem *Rite of Spring,* though disallowed
in lessons, revealed the thrill of ambiguity in its suggestion
of the carnal; a stark rite of passage. Today I'll stow your verse in the bow
of my craft, guard your *Door into the Dark*, a treasured first impression.
I'll row rhyme to the centre of October, then further into open water
to catch a zephyr, to drift the lake's cool-blue afternoon.
Here, a scribbled sky's unstrung pearl slips through its border,
and watermarked, mimics moon. There, a skein of geese assumes
the rusty air of the potting-shed door, their rising path oblique.
But, being no longer here nor there, I must find you
now in *Opened Ground*, take up your *Postscript* and speak
your words to Clare's wild shore where, due
west on Slieve Aughty, a *stony up-againstness* is halting
time at Bohatch Dolmen, where they appear, *all standing waiting*

Omar Sabbagh

To The Middle Of Love

Seamus Heaney, Rest In Peace

Though you never knew me, more than a knowing nod
From the TV; though you near-wept as you read
About your father, a blackbird, and more, much more;
And though you were the festival in your finite life,
Now stroll, beyond all wanderings, naming no error
In those halcyon gardens where all are careless with their
Care; now amble, don't hesitate, there the poems are quiet
As fires without denizens, or hasty feelings for the air
In which they billow, yellow, red, blue as an apple-core.
No. You are not dead, spent, gone. You are
What the birds sing at hallowed morning, knowing the more
In store, knowing what good speed, what loaded dares
Are meant by the passing of a bard to the middle
Of everything. To the middle of love. That's all.

Sudeep Sen

Searching for Seamus

   Today on Sandymount Strand
I looked for you, as you did

   for your *father's ashplant*
many years ago.

   I don't know why I went
on this search

   knowing full well
you weren't there,

   but elsewhere gracing a shoot
'plunging through glar

   and Glitty Sheughs'.
But the script for me

   remains unfinished ...
the dotted line of words,

   of memory, of epiphany,
is something I know

   tide won't wash away.
The secret lies

   in accepting word's own
intent, one that scripts

     one's own fate, with its
  desire, fatality,

   unpredictability,
and its elocuted magic.

Patricia McCarthy

Death of a Bard

To Seamus Heaney

i

Here you very nearly came to stay,
your scribbles to plant new hedges
in the Domesday fields, your perfect pitch
to be learnt by nightingales on the ridge.
'Have a drink,' I can almost hear you say –
'to take the shyness off you': host
to the hostess, myself changed to a guest,
in your own generous, unspoilt way.
The owls will flute you now in the still
of deepest night, your words selve
on every earth's horizon, rooms warmed
by your fire in absence's sudden chill.
No sectarian borders where you delve
space with a pen, etymologies fresh-formed.

ii

Noli timere: yours the echo now
In the layered leaves of every bible:
Guiding, through stone ages, the quills
Of John, Isaiah, Saint Jerome.
Walking on water you take your bow
Re-inventing Latin – church, classical –
In tide-lines, sky-screens all digital,
The swing of the sea your sudden home.
Can you hear the gulls conjugating
New declensions, old staves
Of sight-read notes black as nuns
Offering Gregorian chants, awaiting
Your tuning fork? Pipers dismissed, you brave
Rivalries of angels with your Annunciation.

The Green Knight

William Bedford

Counting the Syllables: Paul Muldoon as Librettist

Shining Brow (Faber, 1993)
Vera of Las Vegas (The Gallery Press, 2001)
Bandanna (Faber, 1999)

Objections to the libretto as a literary form are too well known to rehearse here in any detail. Yeats's complaint 'What was the good of writing a love-song if the singer pronounced love "lo-o-o-o-o-ve?"' [1] or Stravinsky's dismissive 'in setting words to music, the words themselves do not matter, only the syllables' [2] seem to leave little room for the hopeful librettist. But Paul Muldoon is not a poet to be daunted, his faith in serendipity a splendid cover for what in fact is a tremendous creative brio. And if he ever needed it, Muldoon had a model to follow in Craig Raine's *The Electrification of the Soviet Union*, Raine's own venture into the minefield. Dismissing Auden's doubts about sensible people bursting into song – they do after all burst into blank verse in some of our greatest drama – Raine goes on to argue that 'perhaps opera is the only place where poetic drama can now seem obviously natural' [3]. Brecht and Weill are the obvious ghosts at this feast, collaborators who gave equal weight to both words and music, using the language 'of contemporary speech ... full of popular idiom' [4]. In these terms, what we should be looking for is aesthetic seriousness rather than probability.

Muldoon does start off with an advantage. Eliot famously advised Tippett to write his own libretti, but most librettists have been commissioned to work from existing texts – translations or poems and novels chosen for some private reason of the composer, as with Britten. From his first libretto *Shining Brow* – where the only condition laid down by Daron Aris Hagen was that he produce a work based on the life of Frank Lloyd Wright – Muldoon has been free to create his own dramatic situations as platforms for the music, a freedom he exercised in full measure in *Vera of Las Vegas* and *Bandanna*. This may explain why, as David Wheatley argues, all three libretti 'take as their theme the meetings of worlds – meetings, in all three cases, with dangerous and tragic consequences' [5]. Given such freedom, it is no surprise to find that Muldoon's libretti are as referentially rich and imaginatively headlong as his poetry. Even working in collaboration, Muldoon remains recognizably Muldoon, the first clue I think that something different is going on here.

To make a drama out of 'the poetry of architecture' (*Shining Brow*, p.2), Muldoon chose to focus on the personal and professional crises which beset

Wright during the years 1903 to 1914: the breakdown of his relationships with his wife Catherine and his mentor Louis Sullivan. In his obsession with his work, Wright acknowledges that he has 'been a traitor / to my wife, my friends, to architecture' (*ibid*, p.46), but insists that the 'artist must take a harder / and higher road' (*ibid*, p.49) 'beyond / the "average" laws of "average" men' (ibid). But in betraying Catherine with his new lover Mamah Cheney, he merely goes on to repeat the same pattern, as Kierkegaard might have predicted, barely noticing the life around him. His mentor, his *Lieber Meister*, also feels betrayed, Wright beginning his creative life as Sullivan's 'pencil in my hand' (*ibid*, p.1) but going on to international fame as Sullivan sinks into obscurity. But perhaps, for an artist, the more serious betrayal is of the art itself. Appropriating Native American lore in all his talk of architecture, Wright insists that 'form and function are one' (*ibid*, p.5), upon 'form following function' (*ibid*, p.1), and upon architecture as 'a lesson in harmony' (*ibid*, p.4) and 'integral' (*ibid*, p.5). The integral refers to landscape, the great house he builds, Taliesin, supposedly growing out 'of' and not 'on' (*ibid*, p.48) the natural materials and contours of the land, as in Native American practice. But the house is a labyrinth, the Minotaur at its heart a native of another culture, the chef Carleton, who is brutally sacked by Wright, only to return and destroy both house and Mamah and her children. Left alone with his hubris, on the area of stage previously occupied by Sullivan, Wright retreats into fantasy: 'That Mamah's dead and gone / is itself a grand illusion' (ibid, p.85), and perhaps with the words which have recurred throughout *Shining Brow*: 'For everything that's built / something is destroyed' (*ibid*, p.34). There is a headlong momentum to the drama of *Shining Brow* which can be felt even on the page, partly due to the narrative drive of events, and partly to the flexible and naturalistic use of dialogue. And the text has all the referential exuberance we associate with Muldoon's poetry. Even in his childhood, Wright thought of himself as an Ibsenite 'Master Builder,' and has fantasy patrons he calls *La Belle Dame sans Merci* and *The Lady of Shalott*. Mamah translates Goethe's 'Hymn to Nature,' Joyce's 'The Dead' and Yeats's 'Nineteen Hundred and Nineteen' figure, and Coleridge's 'The Rime of the Ancient Mariner' haunts the theme of betrayal. Despite the longings of the characters, there is indeed no Balm of Gilead in the tragedy of *Shining Brow*.

Shining Brow was one of the most successful American operas of the last century, and seems to have freed Muldoon's imagination for the cross-dressing riot of *Vera of Las Vegas*. Here, the verse is free and the naturalistic dialogue could be recitative, the speech-like singing which is written in ordinary notation but with some freedom of rhythm and pitch. In *Shining Brow* the occasional octosyllabic line seems to be handled with an uncharacteristic uncertainty, unlike Raine's use of the same line in *The Electrification of the Soviet Union*. But there is no uncertainty about the narrative drive of *Vera of Las Vegas*. The key source for the libretto is Neil Jordan's *The Crying Game*, the context the Troubles of recent Irish history, though the headlong brutality of the humour reminded me more of Pinter's *The Birthday Party* than any other allusions in the text. The narrative involves two fugitive IRA men, Dumdum and Taco, who find themselves detained in Las Vegas, capital of the rhinestone-clad king Elvis. They are immediately picked up by Doll, a blackjack dealer turned undercover agent for the Immigration and Naturalization Service. Another undercover agent, Vera of the LAPD, is also after Dumdum and Taco, along with two British MI5 assassins, Trench and Trilby, following them from Belfast. Vera is a beautiful black female, Trench and Trilby males in ludicrous disguise which immediately gives them away. Nothing in this world of classical myth and U2's album *The Joshua Tree* is what it seems, the text throbbing with innuendo and the songs of Robert Johnson, gaming tables, slot machines, strippers and chorus girls. Even Dumdum's name gives the game away, so to speak, a dumdum being a soft-nosed bullet that expands on impact. Dumdum and Taco are fleeing justice, or revenge, and as they cross continents, the instability of identity propels the heart of the narrative, Vera turning out to be a man just as Dil is a man in *The Crying Game*, and the two British agents Trench and Trilby in fact revealing themselves to be women. There are too many allusions in the text to mention them all, but at random they include Purcell's *Dido and Aeneas*, Stravinsky's *Oedipus Rex*, Shelley's 'Ozymandias,' the 'Anna Livia Plurabelle' chapter of *Finnegans Wake* and the film version of *Death in Venice*. Helóise and Abelard, Virgil and a passing reference to 'the heart of darkness' (*Vera of Las Vegas*, p. 27) figure, and Hippolyta as a new casino on the Strip. In a moment of cautious political realism, Taco quotes Lao Tzu's famous wisdom 'He who knows does not speak / He who speaks does not know' (ibid, p.49). This may sound like overload, but it certainly does not read like that, every allusion deepening the political themes, creating a dark world where characters exchange sexual identities in their efforts to escape their own fates and guilts, and Taco is left alone on the stage at the end, holding what is obviously an explosive device, the ticking of the bomb ending with the 'judder of the blood and the shudder of a plane taking off' (ibid, p. 53). Black humour which constantly reminded me of Joe Orton, this is political drama of a very high order.

Set in the liminal borderlands of the US-Mexican border, *Bandanna* has the film *noir* darkness of Orson Welles's *Touch of Evil*, the linguistic passion of Lowry's *Under the Volcano*, and the plot of *Othello*. Lorca's *Bodas de Sangre, Yerma* and *La Casa de Bernarda Alba* are also part of the atmosphere of this brooding Day of the Dead, along with the war experiences of two of the main characters in Vietnam and Cambodia. Just as with *Shining Brow* and *Vera of Las Vegas*, we are travelling again in the borderlands of extreme experience. Morales, the Latino chief of police of a tiny town on the border of the US and Mexico is obviously the Othello figure, but in the disguise of the chief of police in Welles's brooding *Touch of Evil*. His white lieutenant Jake is the Iago figure, jealous of the recently appointed Irish-American captain, Cassidy. It is Jake who persuades Morales that Cassidy is having an affair with Morales's wife Mona. Jake's Latino fiancée Emily takes the Emilia role, and there is a labour organizer who adds a political dimension to this borderland world of illegal immigrants: his name Kane being a nice gesture to Welles. And the political dimension is important, adding an ambitious dimension to the narrative. In an important solo, the labour organiser Kane sings of Marx being 'out of favour today / because of the Commie thing' (*Bandanna*, p.24), Cambodia and Vietnam and the assassinations of the Kennedys and Martin Luther King (*ibid*, p.25), Mao's *Little Red Book* (*ibid*, p.26) and Mayor Daley and the Chicago riots at the 1968 Democratic Party Convention (*ibid*, p.28). The verse in *Bandanna* is handled with familiar Muldoonian delight in the serendipity of rhyme, from the chorus of the Townspeople – 'on the Day of the Dead, / *Dia de los Muertos*, / when the living break bread / with Coronado and Cortés' (*ibid*, p.5) – to Mona's version of Desdemona's 'Willow Song' – 'Till the alder sees the willow / as being quite steadfast / after all? The gibbet and the gallows / could not look more aghast' (*ibid*, p47). From the 'riot of excitement in the cantina' (ibid, p.35) at Jake and Emily's wedding reception to the deafening chorus of 'Paramedics, Townspeople, the Dispossessed and the Disappeared' (ibid, p.52) when Morales 'puts the pistol to his mouth and fires' (*ibid*), *Bandanna* creates a drama of borderland crossings against which the tragedy of love and jealousy works its relentless story.

It is obviously the case that libretti are written to be performed. Academic study of theatrical conventions in the Elizabethan theatre has deepened our understanding of Shakespeare and his contemporaries immeasurably. On the page, we miss the gestures which bring the drama to life. So with libretti, where 'simultaneity of events'[6] is the whole point, on the page we miss the musical form which is the expression of the content. With *Shining Brow*, the aural effect of having a soprano, tenor, bass and high lyric baritone taking the lead roles can only be experienced, not imagined. Chorus passages are central to both drama and themes, and it is impossible to *hear* the librettist's intentions when characters in trios or duets are all singing different words. We can all presumably imagine the visual effects of having a chorus of casino girls, strippers and lapdancers cavorting around the stage, but when they comment upon the drama in *Vera of Las Vegas*, the pulsating 'bump and grind' (*Vera of Las Vegas*, p.33) of the music is inevitably lost. There is a Mariachi Band in Bandanna, adding immeasurably to the excitement of the action, trios and duets raising the same problems mentioned above, and a sextet playing a dizzying selection of dance music, from the waltz, pasodoble and beguine to tango, 50s rock and samba. Reading can never bring this completely alive on the page. But then nobody pretends it can. Libretti which can be read to any extent as independent works of literature are rare indeed, excepting perhaps da Ponte and Hofmannsthal, or Brecht and Weill in our own time. With his unique imaginative gifts, and in the circumstances under which he collaborated with Daron Aris Hagen, it seems to me that Muldoon has come as close as any librettist I have encountered.

---

[1] W.B. Yeats, *Essays and Introductions* (Macmillan, 1961) p.14.

[2] W.H. Auden, *Forewords and Afterwords* (Faber & Faber, 1979) p.433.

[3] Craig Raine, 'Preface,' *The Electrification of the Soviet Union* (Faber & Faber, 1986) p.15.

[4] W.H. Auden, *The Dyer's Hand* (Faber & Faber, 1975) p.484.

[5] David Wheatley, '"All Art is a Collaboration": Paul Muldoon as Librettist', *Paul Muldoon: Critical Essays,* Eds. Tim Kendall and Peter McDonald (Liverpool University Press, 2004), p.151.

[6] Kendall and McDonald, ibid, p.155.

Neil Powell

Britten's Books

Benjamin Britten wasn't a particularly fluent or imaginative writer. The diary he kept as a young man is for the most part a busy life's pedestrian aide-mémoire, while his letters often shy away from eloquence: writing home from Italy in 1934 to report his first sight of lakes and snowy mountains, he adds, 'As you notice, I cannot describe it.' Yet he had a very literary cast of mind: his mental library, founded on wide and eclectic reading as a schoolboy and as a music student, would serve him well when he came to choose poems for song-cycles and texts on which to base operas.

During the last term he spent at prep school in 1928, the fourteen-year-old Britten began his 'Quatre Chansons Françaises', which he finished that summer. They are remarkable both for their musical sophistication and for the choice of texts by Victor Hugo and Paul Verlaine which he'd found in *The Oxford Book of French Verse*: the third song, Hugo's 'L'Enfance', about a child who continues to sing and play while his mother is dying, has a nursery-rhyme motif which becomes steadily more compromised and melancholic, in the spirit of creative re-imagining which the composer would later bring to his folk-song arrangements. Britten had already sensed how the French language could act as a filter or a mask, enabling him to treat material too powerful or too personal to handle in English; he'd return, much more knowingly, to this strategy when he came to set Rimbaud in *Les Illuminations*. During his two years at Gresham's School, Holt, he became something of a Francophile, as well as a committed modernist, reading Proust's 'absolutely fascinating' *Swann's Way* while admiring Picasso and listening to Schoenberg: avant-garde tastes which marked, as they often do, the public schoolboy who didn't quite fit.

Nevertheless, when he went at sixteen to the Royal College of Music, a reaction set in: he developed a fondness, tinged with nostalgia and eroticism, for old-fashioned school stories such as F.W. Farrar's *Eric, or Little by Little*, Hugh Walpole's *Jeremy at Crale* and H.A. Vachell's *The Hill*. But the novel to which he returned (reading it 'for the umpteenth time' in May 1932) was *David Copperfield*, a book about both corrupted childhood innocence and his beloved East Anglian coast. Much later, he told Charles Osborne that he'd seriously considered turning it into an opera. He was indeed capable of filing away such ideas for twenty years or more: that very month, he heard on the radio 'a wonderful, impressive but terribly eerie & scary play', a dramatisation of Henry James's *The Turn of the Screw*. Meanwhile, he was reading – and setting to music – such resolutely unmodernist contemporary poets as W.H. Davies, Walter de la Mare and Robert Graves. There's no evidence that he'd come across *The Waste Land*, for instance, and he'd yet to discover the work of a young poet, recently published by Faber, whose name was W.H. Auden.

When Britten met Auden in 1935, he found him 'the most amazing man, a very brilliant & attractive personality'. They were to work together at the GPO Film Unit, collaborating on documentaries such as *Night Mail* and *The Way to the Sea*, as well as on Group Theatre productions and cabaret songs; but for Britten their most significant joint project was *Our Hunting Fathers*, of which he said 'it's my op. 1 alright', although obviously it wasn't. Here, Auden's prologue and epilogue frame poems by Thomas Weelkes and Thomas Ravenscroft as well as the anonymous 'Rats Away' which alone was enough to terrify the audience at the work's Norwich première: there's a strong sense of two clever young men trying to upset their elders and succeeding. Auden was, of course, a crucial part of a leftish-creative metropolitan milieu, which was where Britten, as a jobbing freelance composer, also had to be even if it didn't quite suit him. Despite their shared educational background, political sympathies and sexuality, the two men weren't kindred spirits: the hedonistic, bohemian Auden never understood the way in which Britten's creativity was nourished rather than inhibited by his knotted-up puritanism. When he read *Mr Norris Changes Trains* by '(Auden's friend) Christopher Isherwood', Britten primly noted that 'he over accentuates the importance of the sex episodes'; Auden and Isherwood thought that Britten could do with some 'sex episodes' of his own and blunderingly tried to arrange some. In the end, it was Isherwood rather than Auden who quietly yet decisively influenced two of the composer's finest works, sending him as presents the copy of Hardy's *Collected Poems* from which he chose the texts for *Winter Words* and, with equal prescience, Edmund Blunden's edition of Wilfred Owen just as he was beginning the *War Requiem*.

Auden wondered of love: 'Will it alter my life altogether?' It certainly did in Britten's case. His relationship with Peter Pears was solid and enduring because it was underpinned by creative partnership: from 1939 until his death in 1976, the overwhelming majority of his compositions for solo voice were for Pears (and the main exceptions were for the finest singers of the time, Dietrich Fischer-Dieskau and Janet Baker). The Rimbaud song cycle *Les Illuminations* is a special case, inspired by Wulff Scherchen and performed by Sophie Wyss before it became unequivocally Pears's property. The Keatsian 'Young Apollo', from the same year, is a similar hybrid, conceived out of Britten's infatuation with Scherchen, completed in America with Pears, infused with 'such sunshine as I've never seen before'.

Les Illuminations was followed by *Seven Sonnets of Michelangelo* – 'after Rimbaud in French I feel I can attack anything' – in which the difficulty of the language again masks the intimacy of the poetry: Pears and Britten courageously gave the first performance, soon after their return to England in 1942, at Wigmore Hall, in a recital which seemed to announce more than a musical partnership. But the 'Serenade for tenor, horn and strings' (1943) was a different sort of project, its instrumentation influenced by Britten's radio work with Dennis Brain and its literary content by his friendship with Edward Sackville-West. Here, the poems form an eclectic small personal anthology: although Britten, when he couldn't compose, later developed the habit of taking and opening books from his shelves at random, four of these texts – 'Blow, Bugle, Blow' (Tennyson), the anonymous 'Lyke-Wake Dirge', 'Hymn to Diana' (Jonson) and 'Sonnet: To Sleep' (Keats) – come from a copy of Quiller-Couch's *Oxford Book of English Verse* he'd won as a school prize in 1930. He may already have known Blake's 'The Sick Rose', but it's likely that Sackville-West introduced him to the stanzas from Charles Cotton's 'Evening Quatrains' which so magically follow the horn's Prologue.

The composer as quirky anthologist, juxtaposing familiar and neglected poems, reappears in works such as *A Charm of Lullabies* (Blake, Burns, Thomas Randolph, John Philip, Robert Greene), *Spring Symphony* (Anonymous, Spenser, Thomas Nashe, Peele, Milton, Herrick, Vaughan, Auden, Richard Barnfield, Blake, Beaumont and Fletcher) and *Nocturne* (Shelley, Tennyson, Coleridge, Middleton, Wordsworth, Owen, Keats, Shakespeare). Britten's method is doubly transformative, both illuminating the poems and implying unexpected relationships between them; the listener learns to expect a troubled centre flanked by something more celebratory, with an ambiguously poised conclusion. *The Spring Symphony*, in particular, seems to be ending on a note of raucous C-major optimism until, on the words 'I cease', the music vanishes like an interrupted dream: it's a musical joke of which Haydn might have been proud, except for its bleakness. Britten said that the experience of his 1945 concert tour of Germany (including Belsen) with Yehudi Menuhin 'coloured everything' he subsequently wrote: this predominantly sombre texture informs *The Holy Sonnets* of John Donne, composed immediately after their return, the *Songs and Proverbs* of William Blake and, of course, the *War Requiem*, interleaving passages from the *Requiem Mass* with Owen's poems, which the composer described as 'a kind of reparation'. But there is unconditional joy to be found in the later works written at least partly for children, such as the wonderfully affirmative *Noye's Fludde*, based on the Chester miracle play.

The poet who spoke most directly to Britten, and whose 'wonderful, touching poems' he set in *Winter Words*, was Thomas Hardy, with whom he shared an English rootedness, an intense humanity and a deep understanding of melancholia. At about the same time, he read *Jude the Obscure*, finding much of his own young self in the nature-loving, culturally ambitious boy whose 'dreams were as gigantic as his surroundings were small'. The songs resonate with echoes of his own childhood, especially the two about rail travel: 'Midnight on the Great Western', with its 'journeying boy', and 'At the Railway Station, Upway', with its poignant trio of characters – the convict, the constable and the 'little boy with a violin' (although in Britten's case it had been a viola). 'Proud Songsters' owes something to Britten's competitive streak: he was spurred on when he learnt that Finzi had also set it, a contest without a clear winner but one which provides an intriguing comparison between outstanding setters of English verse at work on the same text. The final song, 'Before Life and After' invoking a time beyond memory, 'When all went well', is perhaps the single poem closest to Britten's heart; its opening words were to become the title of his last work for orchestra, the 'suite on English folk tunes', *A Time There Was*.

This range of poetry set by Britten in his major song-cycles is already colossal; and then there are choral works, including the Hymn to St Cecilia (Auden) and *Rejoice in the Lamb* (Christopher Smart); the church canticles (Francis Quarles, Edith Sitwell, T.S. Eliot); the cycles of untranslated poets such as Hölderlin and Pushkin; the cantata for Janet Baker, *Phaedra* (Robert Lowell's version of Racine); dozens of individual songs and occasional pieces; and, of course, the operas. It was reading about Crabbe while in California – and then reading his poem 'The Borough' – which brought Britten back to Suffolk and altered the course of twentieth-century music in England. It's hard now to appreciate the audacity of Joan Cross, the director of Sadler's Wells, in marking her house's postwar re-opening with a new opera about a deranged East Anglian fisherman, by a living composer who was widely known to be a homosexual and a pacifist. But the public and (for the most part) the critical reception fully justified her risk-taking, and *Peter Grimes* rapidly acquired a reputation well beyond the arts world: a bus-conductor in Rosebery Avenue would call out to his passengers, 'Sadler's Wells! Any more for Peter Grimes, the sadistic fisherman?'

Almost all Britten's operas do extraordinary things with improbable and often intractable literary sources. For instance, *Albert Herring* transplants a comic story by Maupassant to a Suffolk village; *The Turn of the Screw* reworks the Henry James novella which had been so long in Britten's mind but in which, problematically, the pivotal character is either a ghost or an imaginary figment; *A Midsummer Night's Dream* reinvents the play and retains Shakespeare's language throughout. Yet it's the triptych of sea operas – *Grimes*, *Billy Budd* and *Death in Venice* – which, for me at least, stands above the rest. Turning Meville's unyielding, historically-encumbered tale *Billy Budd* into an opera was a tall order even for Britten (and his librettists E.M. Forster and Eric Crozier); staging a piece with an all-male cast, set on an eighteenth-century man o'war, was a tough challenge even for Covent Garden; yet the work is a triumph, of such inwardness and subtlety that Ian Bostridge has suggested it may indeed benefit from being heard on disc, away from the visual distractions of the opera house.

Death in Venice, like *The Turn of the Screw*, had been in Britten's mind for years: it posed the greatest problem of all, as it's essentially a dramatic dialogue in which one of the characters, Tadzio, doesn't speak (and so can hardly be expected to sing). The solution – making Tadzio a dancer, choreographed by Frederick Ashton, while eliding almost all the minor characters into a single role for baritone – placed an enormous burden on the ageing Peter Pears as Aschenbach in the early productions and resulted in a chamber opera of unsurpassed intensity. But perhaps the most remarkable aspect of *Death in Venice* is its strangely glowing subtext of thanksgiving and reconciliation: even as Tadzio walks into the water at the end of the opera, the orchestral colours are, almost reassuringly, those in which Britten had habitually painted the sea. In the libretto by Myfanwy Piper, there's at least one allusion to Virginia Woolf's *To the Lighthouse*; and one can imagine Britten, like his Aschenbach, sharing the sense of exhausted completion felt by the painter Lily Briscoe on that book's final page: 'Yes, she thought, laying down her brush in extreme fatigue, I have had my vision.'

Nigel Jarrett

Auden, Stravinsky and *The Rake's Progress*

Composers have often chosen third-rate poetry to create first-rate vocal music. The history of art song is replete with it. Few other than devotees remember Ludwig Rellstab's poems but far more know the silk purses Schubert made from them. Words and music do sometimes meet on equal terms, among the finest examples in this country being Britten's song settings of W. H. Auden. Their union in opera does not always result from the composer's choice of a pre-existing text but from a collaboration between composer and writer, who may base his libretto on one. They set out jointly to create something in which they both have a stake. In the case of Richard Strauss and Hugo von Hofmannsthal, the impetus often came from the wordsmith. In one important sense, *Der Rosenkavalier* could not have been imagined without the story provided for it by the librettist, the magical pre-nuptial ceremony of the silver rose, with its suggestion of historical precedent, being a fabrication.

Composer with poet would appear to be a welcome pairing, even though the librettist has to attend to narrative as well as lyrical quality. Britten's song settings of Auden are so memorable that many wish the two had combined to write more than one opera. *Paul Bunyan* fairly crackles with Auden bravura, but Britten chose several librettists for his other operas. Auden, in any case, was about to find his greatest fame as a librettist with Igor Stravinsky in *The Rake's Progress*. Its points of departure were the engravings of Hogarth's paintings of that collective title but its centre of operations was America. Auden had notoriously fled Britain for the States before the war. Britten had also decamped there with Peter Pears and then returned – to revolutionise British opera in Britain with his and Montagu Slater's *Peter Grimes*.

Stravinsky saw the Hogarth prints at the Chicago Art Institute in May 1947. Their presentation as scenes from a dramatic life appealed to him in the terms of an interesting operatic form and, being English with a London setting, they were just what he'd been looking for as the subject of an opera in English. He'd been in America for eight years, an exile twice removed from his native Russia. Another exile, Aldous Huxley, had suggested Auden to him as a potential librettist, and there was to be a further collaboration, that of Auden with his friend Chester Kallman. It was Stravinsky who'd introduced Auden to opera. But when we look for the significance of the poetic voice in a libretto, it's important to heed Auden's dictum that 'it is the librettist's job to satisfy the composer, not the other way around'. Auden deferred to Stravinsky from the start, even sketching the libretto in French. One might expect, therefore, to find in Auden's text some suppression of a full poetic flowering in pursuit of narrative flow. But there was poetry in everything Auden wrote. In any case, opera stories are stop-go affairs: characters are for ever halting the action to reflect on what's happening. It's the nature and form of the reflections that can allow the poet-librettist to open out.

It's important to remember that Auden and Kallman had to make a story out of a series of pictures, however indicative the visuals were of an irresistible narrative. They expand Hogarth's bare chronicle to include a lover for the eponymous Rakewell. Also introduced is the devilish Nick Shadow. The story in summary is that Rakewell woos Anne Trulove in an idyllic setting but turns down her father's offer of a lucrative position in the City. Shadow intervenes, accompanies the fleshpot-chasing Rakewell to London as his manservant, grants him three wishes (for riches, for happiness and for an Utopian device to turn stones into bread), bargains unsuccessfully with him for his soul when his investments collapse, then turns him into a madman who believes he is Adonis. In Bedlam, poor Tom is visited by Anne – his 'Venus' – but her ministrations are unavailing. Her father takes her home; a heartbroken Tom dies. Samuel Johnson might have seen it all as an example of the vanity of human wishes.

Auden recognised Hogarth's tableaux as illustrations of the opposite of an established literary form: the story of the Virtuous Apprentice, who does everything right, marries his master's daughter and lives happily if uneventfully ever after. It's a story in which is embedded a moral cliché: that of the idle hands for which the Devil will always find work. Auden also acknowledged that the background to Hogarth's depictions was as bourgeois as its obverse in the sense that what Tom was throwing away were the opportunities afforded jointly by a family legacy (Shadow's doing) and nepotism. Hogarth's is thus a cautionary tale that's familiar enough today as it was in historical settings where mercantile growth dependent on risk and financial reward left the trader open to temptation, self-indulgence and ruin. For Auden, Shadow is not an intellectual concept like Mephistopheles in Goethe's *Faust* any more than Rakewell is an embodiment of evil like Don Giovanni in da Ponte's libretto for Mozart. He's just an incorrigible lad who can't resist temptation of the sort that will leave him penniless and deranged. Debauchery's morally neutral so as long as it doesn't lead to one's material downfall. It's the madness that's eventually unalterable and to be avoided at all costs.

There's an unprepossessing side to Auden's and Stravinsky's American venture. The Russian revolution had driven the composer to Paris, where the cabal of comically-furious French and others who'd revolted at the premiere of *The Rite of Spring* forced him to leave for America, specifically

Los Angeles. His wife, Vera, hated the place; her insecure husband, fearful of poverty, simply wanted to be in the right spot in the event of war or more social upheaval. Kallman, Auden's lover, was raffish, a model of infidelity and an inconsiderable writer. Some see their libretto as too clever, its moral hackneyed, its characters two-dimensional, its dramatic trajectory guided by reason, not emotion. The grim tale, Hogarth's at first, appealed to composer and poet because their outlooks were pessimistic and reactionary. Stravinsky would have identified Hogarth's *mise-en-scène* as ideal for further indulging his neo-classical preoccupations while the anxious Auden, not long before depressed by dives and low dishonesty and now moved by the ravages of war, had done what many English public-school chaps did in a moral crisis and become an Anglican again.

Out of all this – the shared certainty of a masterpiece in the making by two celebrities enervated by a drab post-war world in a meretricious land – came an opera whose libretto, *ipso facto*, has little ponderous undertow. The late Forties were infected more with moral cynicism than lofty thought. The opera was premiered in Venice in 1951. Although both composer and librettist would live on until the 1970s, active political considerations of the future, probably none in Stravinsky's case, were for younger men. Also, it's no coincidence that Auden had helped revive popular English verse and restore it to the literary canon. His libretto's inventiveness (not least the camp creation of Baba the Turk, a bearded woman), its *verismo* portrayal of Augustan rough-and-tumble and its appropriation of the Faust story without the trappings give it the clear directness that Stravinsky probably wished for. So that its poetry, or the poetic qualities of its poet-creator, could be appreciated without too much distraction. The estimate is in the reading and the listening.

Simon Jenner

Comic Operas and The End of Civilisation

Two comic operas about fifteen years apart, two tragic endings encoded in them. Strauss's *Capriccio* and Bernstein's *Candide* may seem from utterly different and certainly distinct musical worlds, and the latter one seemingly brought about the collapse of the former, and at the time of Bernstein's writing, was riding high as the World's greatest superpower. Yet both operas record the death of hope, not in the ostensible subject matter but in their handling of an ending.

Strauss first. *Capriccio* is set in a chateau near Paris around 1775. The theme of the opera can be summarized as 'Which is the greater art, poetry or music?' This question is dramatized in the story of a Countess torn between two suitors: Olivier, a poet, and Flamand, a composer. There's little point in dwelling on this as such, since that's not what the tragic bar is about. But two points. First, this is set in 1775, fourteen years before the French Revolution, as Strauss well knew. And second, the idea came from his old friend and Jewish émigré, later suicide, Stefan Zweig (1894-1942) the novelist and librettist Strauss respected most after Hugo Hofmmansthal's death in 1929.

So Zweig committed suicide in the year *Capriccio* was composed, 1942. The same year Strauss tried to visit the concentration camp where his son's parents-in-law, Jews, were incarcerated. 'I've come to take them home,' he said simply. He was laughed at. They were murdered. Strauss kept quiet about much to save his daughter-in-law.

This then was the backdrop to the beginning of paradoxically Strauss's Indian summer which lasted to his death in 1949. For the decade after *Arabella* (1933) nothing he'd written has quite stayed in the repertoire; indeed, much from the 1920s has been neglected too. In what he saw as his end – this was Strauss's last opus number too (85), oddly, enough was Strauss's new beginning. But he saw no future for Germany and German culture. And as he knew it, he was right. After him, the deluge of Stockhausen. Tonal music was compromised with Nazidom: all those Jewish émigré composers who'd survived were now in effect branded decadents yet again by another Aryan aesthetic: paradoxically in part emanating from the Jewish Schoenberg who refused such doctrinaire positions.

The reason I've written this as knowing tragedy is simple music: five bars from the end, the fragrant discussion veering to music's winning the argument comes to an end. Music takes over and the familiar warm bath of Straussian chromaticism does something singular, out of key with itself: the Rococo civilized Europe depicted by Strauss here and celebrated elsewhere in his output (notably *Der Rosenkavalier* and *Bourgeois Gentilhomme*) the music itself lurches to a devastated minor key. It's unmistakable; baffling at first and heartrending. Its message however is quite clear. All this glittering dust, 1775 France, 1942 Germany, and the man who imagined this first, Stefan Zweig, are dead. Bar the 1789 revolution Strauss must have been thinking: first the Nazis and then the bombs. It's explicit enough since the serene string sextet at the beginning of the opera, often performed as a fine separate concert piece, was in effect expanded to 23 strings, and the whole then plunged into the matter of these couple of bars. This is when Strauss composed *Metamorphosen*; thus three years later in 1945 his explicit lament for the loss of all the Weimar civilization and that of Goethe, Mozart, Schiller, Heine, Beethoven, Schubert, and beyond was gone for ever as he thought. The opera houses, some standing for 200 years, were gone; the world of the Rococo that bore *Rosenkavalier* in the 1740s froth of white ceilings glittered in a terrible Messeinware and human dust in Dresden.

If comedy rather than pathos brought this home, it underlined Strauss's curious adherence to the 18th century dictum that everything could be said within a recognized code or framed in a decorum that allows a thirty two year old woman to reliqush a seventeen year-old lover to a girl of his age as in *Rosenkavalier*. In his case, despite personal dangers, his playing with a minor keyed mode was never likely to land him in much trouble. That was true even of the brief shrouded elegy for a dead Jewish friend, perhaps needlessly hounded by his survivor guilt.

Trouble though was what Bernstein encountered in his ostensibly optimistic satire on optimism, *Candide*, which premièred in 1957 at the same time as his immortal *West Side Story*. *Candide*, despite swapping material with this masterpiece, was never going to be as popular, and yet it too is a masterpiece and in some ways more impressive.

This was just after the most traumatic political period of Bernstein's life. Bernstein like his librettists was a left-leaning liberal reared on the New Deal and the quasi-socialist aspirations of an FDR America that took *The Grapes of Wrath* as a bible of action and touchstone of wrongs. Senator McCarthy had moved in on this nexus of socialist, communist and liberal thinking and the rest as we know is hysteria. Not, incidentally, that McCarthy was entirely wrong it turns out: there really were Reds in the White House. It's just that they were too high up (even higher up than his target Alger Hiss) and that McCarthy's ludicrous persecution of the liberal intelligentsia was the perfect gift for the real Soviet spies to thrive. Senator McCarthy was perhaps the finest – because unwitting – Soviet double agent the Soviets ever had; and they appreciated him.

All this didn't help Bernstein and his friends. Over the opera's gestation these included Dorothy Parker, dramatist Lillian Hellman, Bernstein himself, John La Touche most of all, and later on the poet Richard Wilbur. What these writers held in clear view over this period was the Liberal and Utopian America they'd fought for – several literally in the forces after the New Deal years – being eroded by McCarthy's attacks on artists. The Soviet ideal was one many on the American left had cleaved to and painfully cleaved from; still many others, suspicious of that ruthless utopianism, had embraced at least socialism or at any rate the American kind under FDR and the New Deal. FDR's own Vice-President from 1941-45, Henry A Wallace, was smoked out as a closet Socialist, particularly too for his anti-racism rather than his mysticism. He was later nominated for President by the short-lived Progressive Party in 1948.

What this meant for the score was a libretto brimming with wit quite pitched up from Voltaire's original ('What a day, what a day, for an auto da fé'). The style is hope, as was said of F Scott Fitzgerald, the message was almost despair. Yet since the easy cynicism and lessons Candide learns are ameliorated by wonderful melodies, comic situations and fantastic improbabilities, this picaresque narrative doesn't for the most part seem that tragic. We get glimpses (the wonderful aria 'Glitter and be gay') but the burden is on the end. The variously fortunate group have gathered together under Candide's commune, and the yearning, utterly elegiac ending lurches suddenly into a very clear message:

> We're neither pure nor wise nor good;
> We'll do the best we know.
> We'll build our house, and chop our wood,
> And make our garden grow.
>
> Let dreamers dream what worlds they please;
> Those Edens can't be found.
> The sweetest flowers, the fairest trees
> Are grown in solid ground.

There were to be real communes in the liberal 1960s and '70s, but from the perspective of sixty and more years, it seems the witch-finders did their work thoroughly enough for such liberal ideologies never to take firm root, let alone solid ground. We have individual liberties (literally to glitter and be gay) and of course the great Civil Rights bill; otherwise the conservatives and reactionaries, the forces Bernstein fought against heroically, sometimes comically (in Hunter S Thompson's 1969 'Radical Chic', 'Another canapé,

Mr. Panther?') have won. And the chance of a real American civilization, as opposed to pockets of culture, ceased with it. It has not ended in firestorms and city-flattening genocide, but the long-term effects of the death of communal aspiration holds dire consequences for the world under the total capitalism of the globalizers. This seems plangently prefigured in the resignation and passionate melancholy of the end of *Candide*. It's meant to be a somewhat subdued end to a troubling comic opera nobody can quite position. In fact it is heartbreaking.

Eva Salzman

Opera More or Less Seria; or an Ensemble of Perplexity

Poor relation of all literature, poetry is mere servant in the lavishly funded opera world. That this latter art form more than any other requires of me – a poet – the most effort to suspend disbelief might sound like a joke.

I am that philistine who finds opera ridiculous; still I wish to enter the magic realm. Opera – the word alone – prompts in me a peculiar anxiety and what I can only describe as an acute ambivalence. Does not poetry prompt in many the same? Plato, valuing the poets, also threw us out. As they say: it's complicated. Even ardent fans can agree opera is complicated for them too

Composer and critic Everett Helm calls opera 'the problem child' though not because it is elitist, which it is, indisputably ('The Libretto Problem'). What I find most intolerable is the excruciatingly affected not to say dull elitism of the pedantic purist aficionados. I too appreciate, if part-time only, the fact of an art that endures imprisoned in archaism and anachronism. But it has always been a given for me that Glyndebourne or English National Opera's large-scale productions are only part of the story: that part costing more to attend than most poets, including those who serve it, can afford, and which attracts enviably colossal sums of funding. About music too Plato had words, although Book IV's less-than-ambivalent warning could serve as endorsement too, however unwittingly: 'We must guard against adopting new forms of music, because that puts everything we value at risk ...the modes of music never change without also changing the fundamental laws and conventions of society.'

In his essay 'Towards Music Theater', the Vienna-born director Walter Felsenstein states, 'Between the traditional and new in the art of opera production there is war.' He laments shortcomings in the traditional singers' training which does not integrate '... characterization and ... vocal technique'. To 'humanize' stage singing he recommends singers are involved in studying the score because 'actions and characters become fully recognizable and comprehensible only by learning about the situation that existed *before* the start of the play'. Apart from such an idea hardly being novel in the music-theatre world, it is interesting no mention is made of the librettist who is surely in a good position to aid in these inquiries.

Economics limit the quantity of new work the large houses deliver and also its scope. In contrast to northern European countries such as France and Germany there are few opportunities to develop small – and medium-scale work in Great Britain and America. The yearly resurrected standards dominating the large house repertoires, however daring or experimental the staging or interpretation, reiterate opera outside of these as moribund. The few smaller companies depend largely on volunteers who can afford the mostly unpaid luxury of writing for opera.

In these views I must be channeling the ethos and vision of my father, the composer and writer Eric Salzman, long a practitioner and proponent of the new music-theatre in which '...alternatives to grand opera and the popular musical go back at least as far as Schoenberg's *Pierrot Lunaire*, early Stravinsky and Kurt Weill as well as the Broadway and off-Broadway theater operas of the '30s and '40s and the modernist experiments of the '60s.' (*The New Music Theater: Seeing the Voice, Hearing the Body* by Eric Salzman and Thomas Desi – cover). In a 1997 interview at the Maison des Ecrivains my father describes this Music-Theatre as 'the most ancient and the most modern of the arts, the most esoteric and experimental and yet, at the same time, the most popular... In its recent manifestations it is the off-off Broadway of opera'. A good deal of it (even small-scale opera) rejects the grandeur of grand opera for many reasons including the preference for nonprojected voices (extended voice, pop, non-European styles or other kinds of singing that need to be amplified), a desire for audience immediacy, or a general esthetic or philosophical preference for small-scale, unpretentious, small-theatre work.

His life's work, then, assumes an art form remains relevant to the age while it continues to be written by living artists who demonstrate and prove its vitality by actively engaging with the development and renewal of its vernacular.

The childhood score at home, at 29 Middagh Street in Brooklyn, was as eclectic and wide-ranging as my father's compositions and reviewing territory. W. H. Auden, Carson McCullers, Jane and Paul Bowles, and Benjamin Britten and his partner, the tenor Peter Pears, all had once lived at 7 Middagh Street which George Davis rented after seeing it in a dream.

My father's reviews run the gamut from the Baroque to Mozart to the esoteric and off-beat. His compositions range from the atonal to the tonal, from the avant-garde to the more traditional narratives and modern fables written with his collaborator Michael Sahl: for example, *Stauf* – for which read 'Faust' – and *Civilisation and Its Discontents* which won the Prix Italia and, when broadcast on National Public Radio, had one of the largest air plays of any work of its kind. *The Peloponnesian War* was a full-evening solo dance work performed by the iconoclastic choreographer Daniel Nagrin, a family friend with whom I later studied improvisation and choreography. *The Last Words of Dutch Schultz*, its text derived from the transcription of a dying gangster's last words, prompted a critic at its Amsterdam première to muse on the '... Kurt Weill of the 90s'.

The composers Lukas Foss, William Bolcolm and Pierre Boulez and Stephen Sondheim have been in our orbit as dinner guests or attending our regular New Year's parties: this last attending one thrown with producer Kevin Eggers at his Chelsea Hotel apartment. At these social events, musicians, singers and actors often gave impromptu performances, even when sober. I wish I could recall the pianist Charles Rosen's exact words when he visited us. His was a conversation of brilliant monologue to which I listened intently, for all the good it did me. My mother describes a night on the town with Stockhausen, she and my father charged with taking him to hear the latest avant-garde music.

Daily life for this author-as-child provided the example of the routinely insecure, precarious and sometimes downright impecunious bohemian life of the freelance artist. The purpose of education was not primarily to aid the acquisition of a proper job, unless one counts teaching as such which, judging by the pay in Great Britain, most do not. Associate Professor at Queens College for two years, my father gave workshops nationally and internationally, travelling widely starting from his pre-children Fulbright in Europe in 1956 during which time the top floor of our house was rented to Lee Hayes of The Weavers. I recall a succession of broken-down Volkswagen beetles, including ones I cannot possibly recall, such as their first, purchased with $900 wedding money from the Wolfsburg, Germany factory, driven back to Rome mid-winter over snow-covered Alps and later shipped back to the USA. So it could not have been broken at all. That European jaunt is documented by a numerous photos of my mother posing before every major ancient Italian ruin. There is also a shot of them with Max Davies with whom dinners were shared both in Rome and in London.

A good portion of his *Introduction to 20th Century Music* (Prentice-Hall), a leading internationally translated textbook on the subject, was written on the Queen Mary en route to Europe in 1964. (My father says: What else was there to do for 6 days on these big old liners?!) That started our year based in Paris, when my father held a Ford Foundation grant to cover music festivals. A photo from that period shows my parents outside La Fenice opera house in Venice. My mother sits elegantly cross-legged in the midst of a posed pyramid of waiters in bow ties and the founding member composers of the avant-garde group Once – including Robert Ashley and Boucourechliev, a French composer of Bulgarian origin in the Boulez school – all of them looking very 60s Euro-chic, the children by then deported back to America presumably so the parents could have more fun.

This fun included our broken-down beetle being towed by a farmer on a horse-cart into Warsaw from where an urgent telegram went out to composer Eliot Carter whom my parents were to meet in West Berlin. There, the needed part was procured and then shipped via Rotterdam while my parents waited, drank and flirted – or anyway my mother did, by her own admission – with the Polish conductor Andrzej Markowski whose daughters had been born in a concentration camp. At last a call came to their hotel and my parents made their way down to the garage.

'Monsieur,' the mechanic spoke to my father gravely, 'Votre voiture est ... *finie.*'

This terrible news caused parental collapse – or anyway maternal collapse, as my mother puts it – until they both realized he meant simply that the repair was complete. Fortunately, no war hung in the balance, dependent on this mistranslation. The car trundled onwards, surviving my father's Bayreuth master class until, finally and genuinely *finie,* it was abandoned on the lawn of Richard Wagner's villa Wahnfried, presumably with his great-granddaughter Nike's permission. Other handed-down family stories involve quantities of modern music, wine, vodka, the Rumanian National Ballet company and the hotel staff where they were staying who told my parents: 'Lock your door. They steal.'

A decade or so on, my parents and I are sprawled on the lawn of the music camp Indian Hill, alongside the folk singer Judy Collins who had recorded songs and arrangements by Josh Rifkin and by my father's collaborator Michael Sahl who was also her pianist and music director for a time. In this photo I'm leaning back on my hands, trying to look casual and less fat. Mordecai and Irma Bauman were as much an institution as this camp they ran in Stockbridge, Massachusetts in the Berkshires near Tanglewood: she the imperious major domo who scared the shit out of me, frankly and who was, from an earlier marriage, the mother of bassist Chuck Israel who played for Bill Evans. Morty was a bass-baritone singer known for his rendition of songs by Charles Ives and Hans Eisler, a contemporary of Weill's who studied with Schoenberg. (My father recounts how Eisler, a communist, was hauled up in front of The House *Committee* on *Un-American Activities.* His brother, having just escaped this ordeal by taking a Polish ship out of NYC's harbour, subsequently composed the East German national anthem and then for his pains was persecuted by the fascists as well as the communists, which is a double whammy if I ever heard one.)

Reminiscing about Indian Hill more recently, Irma was still sharp and imposing if a little less scary in her nineties. Stan Getz's daughter attended the summer I did although apparently that year produced an unusually large crop of writers including novelist Meg Wolitzer and Isabel Fonseca, author of *Bury Me Standing: The Gypsies and Their Journey* (and also later Martin Amis's wife). After Morty's death Irma penned a memoir about their musical lives and their shepherding of scores of artistically inclined teenagers, many of whom became prominent artists.

Eva's Dad with Boulez

Moving forward in time, there is a photo showing my long-haired father leaning over Pierre Boulez as he prepares my father's *Foxes and Hedgehogs* with the BBC for a Roundhouse concert, the words for this piece derived from the book-length poem *Europe*, by John Ashbery whose writing was also integrated into Steven Wade's text for my father's iconic multi-media work *The Nude Paper Sermon*. William Gibson's article 'Signal to Noise' recounts the thrill of becoming caretaker of a professor's treasure trove of vinyl, his re-discovery of the Nonesuch label and in particular my father's work. A subsidiary of Elektra records, Nonesuch was considered ground-breaking for its early synthesized electronic music and, for example, the Explorer series, which Gibson calls 'the first attempt by a popular American label to record folk music from around the globe ...the progenitor of what we would now call "world music"'. Records my father produced for Nonesuch include *The Tango Project* and the Grammy nominated *Unknown Kurt Weill*, sung by soprano Theresa Stratas (who was, and may still be, partner of the poet Tony Harrison).

Originally a Nonesuch commission and so firstly written to be recorded – the stage version came later – *The Nude Paper Sermon* is widely regarded as in the vanguard of electronic music. In the journal *Cadence* Dustin Mallory calls my father '...a visionary of the future of music theater'. (I just called him Dad of course.) *The Nude Paper Sermon*, Mallory continues, 'blurs the lines of time and genres by mixing the sounds of a Renaissance consort and... Motet singers, with a modern inclusion of electronic sounds and an actor/narrator...[who] positions himself as a media/cultural voice' of that period.

That to which the child is inured does not seen odd or unusual; I had not yet realized anyone thought such music odd or unusual. What did seem odd was how often the musically erudite were unfamiliar with this genre, or discovered it belatedly, if they wished to discover it all, that is. *The Nude Paper Sermon's* environmental and societal allusions are as timely now as they ever were. The piece seems perfectly emblematic of a period's radical societal changes that may be said to have culminated in an anti-war movement transcending age, background and political complexions. The backdrop of my childhood was a transformative culture, its art addressing as a matter of course aspects of itself and all manner of politics.

The Nude Paper Sermon dates from the early 70s which, as we know, was when the 60s really happened. Some of its Nonesuch consort singers subsequently formed the nucleus of my father's music-theatre group Quog, named after the town where the paternal grandparents had purchased a house many years previously. The small troupe of singers/performers would travel out to Quogue for extended days-long rehearsals. Starting from when I was around eleven years old, little was censored in front of the children. Naturally, to be thrown among grown-ups and often treated as one was heady and exciting, confirming my opinion that I was indeed an adult, with the only difference being that I was not allowed to smoke grass (yet).

Mornings, I stepped over sleeping bodies on the living room floor. Someone would put on the record player a Harry Nilsson song that exhorted everyone to wake up and start vocalizing weirdly in the pine and hickory woods. According to our local friends, this was done naked. Apparently, my father's father once chased kids down the path through the woods waving a knife. (It is true that sweeping gesticulations of his cane punctuated the conversations he initiated with neighbours and strangers alike in a way that might have been construed as dangerous.) Like John Cage – beside whom my father stands in another photo taken after a Brooklyn Academy performance – my father is a pretty expert mycologist, as indeed one must be because the inedible ones can kill you.

My mother recounts how during this period Luciano Berio, who was then teaching at Julliard, sailed his boat with his small daughter up the Hudson and through the inland waterway on the south shore, dragging a seine net the whole way. Upon arrival in East Quogue he hung this up outside our house and removed all manner of bizarre sea creatures – including some edible fish – which were then all thrown into a vast pot. He boiled the bejeezus out of the whole mess: the scales, bones and shell then picked out bit by bit from our individual bowls as we ate, murmuring our praises of what Berio assured us was an authentic *zuppa di pesce* from Liguria where he was born.

Unbelievably and disappointingly, my mother denies that she and my father were hippies. Their bringing home upon release each new Beatles album proves nothing, I realize. The Nonesuch Consort's founding members went on to eminent careers that did not entail bad behavior or hallucinogens. Apart from being a pianist and conductor – including of *The Nude Paper Sermon* – Josh Rifkin is a Bach scholar. The baritone Alan Titus achieved operatic fame. The counter-tenor William Zukof went on to form Western Wind, an early music group that later commissioned my father's work *Jukebox in the Tavern of Love* which premièred at the Flea Theatre in Tribeca; he also sang at my first marriage though I doubt this helped his career. Richard Taruskin, the viola da Gamba player has since become a famous – and maverick if not curmudgeonly – musicologist and critic. So far this is respectable, especially the curmudgeonly part.

The poet Ruth Fainlight had been the catalyst for my entry into my father's world when she suggested my participation on an Opera Performing Arts Lab at Bore Place in Kent which entailed an onerous ten days of free food and lodging in a beautiful country estate. I have always assumed that the librettist having some musical knowledge is a benefit in that it affords one a clearer future perspective on potential performance dilemmas and their bearing on the composition process. For example, consideration of voice and instrumentation must be taken into account and might have to trump authorial preciousness. Perhaps less understanding of music can be balanced by a willingness to be flexible, and trust in one's composer collaborator: not always easy to establish in so short a period or in a compressed period of time.

The use of anonymous text fragments is one way to solve the copyright or narrative problem – assuming you consider narrative a problem – and composers are thus spared having to deal with living authors' egos which are as healthy or unhealthy as theirs. In any case, the librettist's place in opera's fixed and implacable hierarchy is perhaps lower even than that of the screenwriter who at least is paid well to write a movie which may never be produced. A joke underlining the writer's lowly place in that industry recounts an apocryphal story about an ambitious blonde bimbo who sleeps with the writer to guarantee her route to stardom.

Happy experiences with the English National Opera Studio were succeeded by perhaps the most dispiriting experience of my writing life: a commission that deteriorated into a time- and energy consuming scuffle over ownership of the original story and characters which was finally solved after union intervention. I should have spotted the warning signals. At our first meeting the ex-teacher director returned my 'homework' with notes; the few pages of a draft foolishly entrusted to him early on were scrawled with corrections of the slant and half rhymes. Practically his first words to me were: 'I'm a writer too.' (My response to this kind of remark generally is to point out that I can carry a tune yet do not believe this makes me an opera singer.) Eventually I was vindicated as regards copyright, but not sent a ticket nor even invited to the performances. The composer's article in the glossy programme about the text's development does not mention me.

Of course in Mozart's day there was no notion of copyright. Once released into the public arena the libretto was fair game and public property, passed around and liberally altered or moulded to suit a composer's purpose or the fashion of the times. He wrote his father that '…in an opera the poetry must be altogether the obedient daughter to the music'. Naturally I am more in accord with the 18th century authority Francesco Algorotti's opinion of the librettist's status. He maintained that the 'poet should be the "creator and director" of the whole – that the composer's function is to give colour and intensity to the words', a view that serious opera buffs would no doubt deride. They would more approve of Everett Helm's allusion to the 'great, perhaps exaggerated importance attached to the libretto' in support of which opinion he cites great works which are not undermined by their admittedly inferior texts. The libretti of *Rigoletto* and *Tosca* he calls 'repugnant'. Famed pre-opera musico-dramatic spectacles range from the 'mediocre to the grisly', including some of Purcell's work.

Referring to the composer's eternal quest for decent libretti, Helm rummages around to explain their inadequacies. The obligatory happy endings in both opera seria and opera buffa distort the story. Italian writing is 'overloaded and disfigured by baroque affectations'. He seems misguided however in blaming made-to-order writing per se. More relevant is the purpose for which the work is written, and for whom. Consider the Poet Laureate's remit producing 'occasional' poetry, which in practice means sucking up to royalty or reeling out a superficial inflated homage to current events.

Only in the 20th century was the libretto seen as literature in its own right, yet literary merit is no assurance of an opera's success. Symbolism may even be a hindrance. Notably, a composer's own libretto, adequate at the very least for his own purposes, would fare less well if set to another's music. Helm says Menotti is one of the few composers whose libretti are universally lauded. Mozart's liberal interventions are regarded as benefitting the work of his collaborator who is widely considered the greatest librettist ever. In a statement about the music/text hierarchy that parallels that of his famed collaborator, Lorenzo Da Ponte said: '... if the words of a dramatic poet are nothing but a vehicle of the notes, and an opportunity to the action, what is the reason that the composer of music does not take at once a doctor's recipes, a bookseller's catalogue, or even a spelling book, instead of the verses of a poet, and make them vehicle to his notes, just as an ass is that of a bag of corn.'

Among our family photos a copy of Da Ponte's death certificate turns up. This flamboyant man's wildly adventurous and unchaste life was itself worthy of an opera. Discovering he had been buried in New York City – which sounds improbable – my father tracked down the site, old St. Patrick's church in Manhattan. A few graves remained but most had long ago been excavated and re-buried in a vast cemetery we have driven past my whole life en route to Quogue. It abuts and is shadowed by a giant power station near the Kosciuszko Bridge which is named after a Polish soldier from Catherine the Great's time who, equally improbably, became a hero of America's war of Independence, thus earning himself the dubious honour of having his name attached to this unlovely bridge arching over a trickle of chemicals that used to be a bucolic stream.

Somewhere below the Brooklyn Queens Expressway overpass, just before it funnels onto the Long Island Expressway, among the vast stretches of jumbled and leaning monuments – the splendid panorama of the midtown Manhattan skyline in the near distance – lies Da Ponte's unmarked grave. Most librettists and poets leave less of a mark. His extraordinary life story ended here, in an ugly part of the city where centuries later another composer drives by with his writer daughter who at this point, during what has always seemed a very long journey, begins to muse on an opera starring Catherine the Great and a strangely misplaced Polish-American war hero of the 18th century, set in the grim industrial wastelands of the borough of Queens.

Above, Eric Salzman with Cage at BAM and below, Eric Salzman and his wife in Rome with Sir Peter Maxwell Davies;

Wasfi Kani

Pimlico Opera is back in prison

It is often said that I am the Robin Hood of the opera world. At one end there is Grange Park Opera – with its magical secret ambience of former times at Glyndebourne – and at the other end is the time spent in prison with Pimlico Opera.

I started Pimlico Opera in the late 80s and there have been twenty-two six-week projects in prison. That is a total of two and half years inside. I had been to school behind Wormwood Scrubs and that is the first prison with which Pimlico Opera collaborated in Sondheim's *Sweeney Todd* in 1991.

In those days the Chief Inspector of Prisons, Stephen Tumim, was making a big splash. He spoke in the poshest voice on the side of prisoners. He died in 2003 and I want him to be remembered for the good sense he spoke: 'If in prison you systematically humiliate a man, he is hardly likely to come out wanting to be a useful member of society.'

All kinds of really grand people were due to turn up to the first night of *Sweeney Todd* but the person the prisoners were most excited about coming was Stephen Tumim. Some of the prisoners saw him as a member of the establishment who had locked them up, but others saw beyond the bow tie, and saw him as someone who was trying to sweep out the prison service. It was 1991 and Stephen was talking about ending slopping out, i.e. the use of buckets as lavatories. 'What?' you are thinking.

It goes like this: prisoners get locked around 7 or 8pm for around twelve hours. Cells in many prisons didn't have lavatories so a bucket was used. In the morning you took your bucket to the wing lavatory and emptied it. Slopping out. This sounds bad enough but there is more: you shared a cell with another prisoner. And you shared a bucket.

Victorian prisons had been built with integral sanitation – a loo in a cell – but as prisoner numbers increased, a cell built for one had to accommodate two and the loo was removed.

Back to Stephen. He was a pretty radical figure. What struck me at that first meeting was how easy he was with the prisoners. He was this pillar of the establishment, and yet prisoners liked talking to him. He was firm, understanding, but not at all condescending. They didn't feel they were talking to just another prison governor. They felt that somehow their voice would be heard beyond the prison walls if they talked to Stephen Tumim. He spoke a lot of common sense.

When I started working in prisons, I didn't know much about prisoners, but my hunch was that you have to do something with these guys. You can't just lock them up and leave them, because for one thing it's very, very expensive, and many are very poorly educated. As the governor of Wandsworth said to me: 'Two thirds of the guys are here because every other government agency has failed.' These are just young men, they are ordinary young men who have done some bad things, but this does not mean they are irredeemably bad people.

Pimlico Opera has enabled both prisoners and the public to participate constructively in a meaningful arts activity in prison. For example, since 1991 we have taken more than 50,000 members of the public into prison; 1,000+ prisoners have participated and 9,000 prisoners have seen a show. The next stretch is two months in Bronzefield Prison, near Heathrow Airport, one of only thirteen UK women's prisons.

The prisoners sign up to six weeks of full-time rehearsal with a professional director, choreographer and a few professional colleagues (mainly the male roles). The final week of rehearsal takes place in the gym which is transformed into a theatre with a lighting rig, raked seating and orchestra pit. Everybody sees they must work hard and aspire to the highest standards. There are seven public performances (Feb 28, March 1, 2, 5, 7, 8, 9) and two other performances for prisoners and prison staff.

Back in the 1990s there were fewer than 2,000 women in prison. Today that figure has doubled. 18,000 children are currently separated from their mothers in prison, as only 5% remain in their own home. A third of children in care end up in prison. A third of women in prison lose their homes, reducing future chances of employment and shattering families. Over half will re-offend within a year of release. Nearly two thirds of boys who have a parent in prison will go on to commit some kind of crime themselves. Of all the women who are sent to prison 37% say they have attempted suicide at some point in their lives. With only 13 female prisons in the UK, women are more likely to be held in custody further away from home. There are 120 male prisons.

Though these statistics are gloomy ... the show isn't. *Sister Act* is the story of lounge singer, Delores, who is on the hit list of a mob boss. She is put under protective custody in a convent where she leads the nuns in gospel, swing and upbeat antics.

The project provides a rare opportunity for prisoners to show themselves, their fellow prisoners and the staff what they can achieve if they put their minds to it. Most importantly, they can show their family for whom it is an emotional event: seeing their relative as the giver of praise – evidenced by audience applause – rather than castigation. This is important as there is no doubt that imprisonment has a huge impact on the family and it is the family who will help develop the support structure for the prisoner's return to a functional life upon release.

The specific learning required for the performance (words, music, their entrances/exits, organsation of props) impacts on other areas of learning: literacy, behaviour and more. And even though the two month project is a long journey for the women, they surprise themselves. Many have never achieved anything of note in their lives. Over the years I have observed that singing and performing build confidence since, even if you can't read, you can learn a song.

Working towards a larger common good is uplifting for the prisoners. They learn through the project that hard work and discipline bring great rewards and that it feels good to achieve ... it's good for your mental health ... it feels better to be on the right track than the wrong track.

The most noble aims would be to keep these women from re-offending, to keep families together, to make these women want to be contributing members of society and not to waste their lives in prison.

A positive experience in prison may just help the chance for each prisoner of successful resettlement on release. The following heartfelt letter from a prisoner's mother shows exactly this:

> I really had to put it in writing to you to say a huge thank you, to you and your company, for many reasons. My son, daughter and myself found the evening truly wonderful and it had a profound effect on us all.
>
> We are just an ordinary family who work hard and have responsible jobs, so as you can imagine, having D 'go astray' has been very hard to deal with at times. Seeing him in this production and hearing all the positive comments on how hard he and all the cast had worked was so inspiring. Watching the whole cast was so professional and it is to your credit what you and your company are doing for these people. Until we came into contact with Pimlico Opera we had no idea such companies existed and wish there were more activities such as yours as I feel it could make a huge difference to these men, who very obviously, in many situations probably haven't been given a chance in life.
>
> It was the best Mother's Day present I have received honestly, and now that D is being transferred to an open establishmen,t we hope this experience will stay with him and help in his rehabilitation to normal life again.
>
> With kind regards K.M., N.M., S.M.

Sister Act in Bronzefield Prison near Heathrow Airport runs Feb 28 - Mar 9, 2014
The Grange Park Opera festival runs May 30 - July 12, 2014
Massenet *Don Quichotte*, Verdi *Traviata*, Britten *Peter Grimes*, Tchaikovsky *Queen of Spades*
www.grangeparkopera.co.uk   info@grangeparkopera.co.uk

Karen Anderson

Glyndebourne's outreach work

The Glyndebourne Festival was founded in 1934 by John Christie and his opera-singer wife, Audrey Mildmay. Today the Festival runs from May to August with a programme of six operas in a world-class 1,200-seat opera house. Together with the Glyndebourne Tour it presents about 120 live performances each year to a total audience of around 150,000. Its resident orchestras are the London Philharmonic Orchestra and the Orchestra of the Age of Enlightenment.

Glyndebourne is committed to reaching and engaging with as broad an audience as possible and throughout 2012 and 2013 has widened its raft of initiatives to grow its audiences. Approximately 20,000 people participate every year in Glyndebourne's rich and varied education programme. This includes youth and community work, subsidised performances for young people, talks and study events. Some of Glyndebourne's recent work in this area includes opportunities for young singers, involves families, young children, under 30s; youth and community work, opportunities for amateur performers from all age groups; special performances for schools, opportunities for local young people age 8-18 to learn key skills for performing and devising opera; chances for the learning disabled community from across the South East to participate in song, music, film and sculpture; involvement with people with dementia and their carers. Glyndebourne has also, since 2007, been a digital pioneer; it screens and broadcasts operas worldwide, offering this art form to people who cannot necessarily get to live performances.

The Glyndebourne Tour began in 1968, with the aim of bringing opera to new audiences and creating performance opportunities for young singers in the Glyndebourne Chorus, as well as for other emerging international singers and conductors. The Tour travels the country every year from October to December. This year it features *Hänsel und Gretel*, *L'elisir d'amore* and *The Rape of Lucretia*.

For the first time, with *Encore* Week, Glyndebourne recently offered a full week of extra performances and events during Tour 2013 aimed exclusively at engaging new audiences – families, children and under 30s.

Glyndebourne's community opera *Imago* was performed on the main stage in March 2013 to great acclaim. An incredibly ambitious project, it featured over 70 amateur performers from teenagers to those in their seventies, working alongside professional soloists; and 25 young musicians working in the orchestra pit playing alongside Aurora Orchestra.

Since 2006, Glyndebourne has offered dedicated Performances for Schools at Glyndebourne as part of their annual Tour, and in 2008 extended the offer to Stoke-on-Trent. Given the success of these performances and the opportunity they provide to engage significant numbers of young people with opera, often for the first time, these have now been taken up in other venues. In 2013, the Performances for Schools programme was extended to include performances for school children in Norwich, Canterbury, Milton Keynes and Plymouth while continuing at Glyndebourne and Stoke-on-Trent. Heavily subsidised, but full length and fully staged, these performances play a crucial role in establishing Glyndebourne's audiences for the future.

Glyndebourne Youth Opera, a project for local young people aged 8-18, works with 120 people across two Youth Opera groups. Participants learn key skills required for performing and devising opera. In December 2012 their work for the year culminated in a main stage performance of *Till the Summer Comes Again*, inspired by Glyndebourne's wind turbine. This year, the GYO project is inspired by the work of Benjamin Britten in a new performance entitled *Into the Harbour, Carry Me Home*. It was staged at Glyndebourne on Friday 22 November 2013 as part of the Britten centenary celebrations nationally.

Inspired by the story of learning disabled athletes returning to London 2012, Glyndebourne's main stage saw the première of a new performance, *Gold Run*, incorporating song, music, film and sculpture, created with and performed by the learning disabled community from across the South East in 2012. This original Glyndebourne commission was developed in partnership with Carousel and Pallant House Gallery.

Glyndebourne Academy was a pilot programme for 2012. Eight gifted young singers aged 18–27 were given unrivalled access to mentoring from singing and performance professionals. These were individuals who, for various reasons, are not able to follow the traditional training routes.

Annually since 2008, Glyndebourne has offered an escape through opera for people with early to moderate-stage dementia and their carers. As well as providing a focus for people facing the challenges of confusion and memory loss, the carers also have an opportunity to share the pressure of caring, and connect with others in similar circumstances. This project, *Raise Your Voice*, is run in partnership with The Alzheimer's Society.

Supported by Glyndebourne's New Generation Programme, the under-30s programme forms part of a drive to introduce opera to new audiences, offering exclusive ticket offers, regular emails, events and dedicated nights to visitors under 30.

Glyndebourne is very much to the forefront digitally, screening and broadcasting operas to a global audience. It hosts operas for free online and screens its own productions into cinemas worldwide. For example, as part of the 2013 centenary celebrations to mark the birth of Benjamin Britten, BBC Radio 3 will broadcast *The Rape of Lucretia* on 28 December, recorded live during Tour 2013 and the Glyndebourne Festival production of Benjamin Britten's *Billy Budd* was shown on television by BBC4 in late November.

The Glyndebourne Festival 2014 will run from 17 May to 24 August, marking the company's 80th anniversary. The 2014 season will feature *Der Rosenkavalier, Eugene Onegin, Don Giovanni, La finta giardiniera, La traviata* and *Rinaldo*.

More information is available from glyndebourne.com

Baldwyns Prayer

David Harsent

The Salt-Wife

Midsummer and late in the day. We met by chance.
Her hair was still wet from the sea. Her dance-steps
were there in the sand, clear-cut as the tide fell back.
She walked along with me. The moon was rising
straight from the long clean line of the horizon,
everything shades of blue
and the pair of us sure-footed across the shingle
towards the house, which showed the single light
I always left on as a beacon in the black.

*

                              That first night
                              I had a dream
                              in which she walked
                              naked beside me
                              on the path
                              up to the house
                              I took her dress
                              wet from the sea
                              and while she slept
                              I hid it then
                              forgot the place
                              as I knew I should

*

Each morning, she went back to where
she had danced that day and swam
a long, clean line from the bay to the vanishing-point
then let the tide bring her back to roll
in the surf. You might think a body had washed-up
in the breakers, but then you'd see her eyes
wide open against the salt. I picked her out,
stone cold. I kissed her mouth, still wet from the sea.

*

>   In this room
>   shreds of darkness
>   hang in corners
>   or they cloud
>   the window where
>   my image is
>   caught between
>   this world and that

*

When the yell went up from headland to headland,
when they were calling the catch,
she would go to the cliff-top. The shoaling fish
ran shallow, a silver swell
heaving against the wavebreak
then a mile-long line of light as they broke the skim.

She would tremble at that …as the boats put out, as they hauled the nets.

*

>   From this window
>   when night comes on
>   shades of blue
>   deepening to black
>   a line of light
>   falls on the sea
>   and rides the swell
>   it's all I see
>   and all I hear:
>   the aftershock
>   of waves against
>   the cliff; it shakes
>   my heart …all I
>   remember is
>   her skin smooth as
>   a washed pebble,
>   the way her tongue

                  would leave a trace
                  of salt between
                  my lips and how
                  her eyes grew dull
                  with sleep as she
                  first slipped my hand
                  then turned from me

        *

There were days when she seemed lost in shades of blue.
If I found her on the shore, close and leaning in,
she would raise a hand to signal silence,
as if there might be voices in the spindrift.

        *

                  When I sit still
                  in this high room
                  from dusk to dawn
                  shreds of darkness
                  unpick to give
                  what seems to be
                  a sight of her
                  somewhere between
                  this world and that.

        *

Midnight. Firelight. The house held in silence.
We both sat still.
Her book lay unopened on her lap.
Darkness dredged on the windowsill like snow.

        *

                  The mystery
                  of how we met
                  comes back to me
                  as waking dreams
                  in which her dance

>   mirrors somehow
>   our lovemaking
>   lightness of touch
>   almost as slight
>   as gestures in air
>   in which moonlight
>   silvers her skin
>   and blanks her eye
>   in which I catch
>   the smell of brine
>   that every night
>   she brought to bed

*

The sea on one side running green against the grey
of outcrop granite, the growl of the undertow;
on the other side
a kestrel holding up against the cliff.
Midday heat on the tideline-rocks set up a shrill
that seemed to hang an inch above the wave-break …

She went a step ahead, seeming to fade
into the haze. Something she said came back to me
on still air, a mix with the insect hum and the shriek of gulls.

*

>   Hour of the rat
>   lightfooted on
>   pelmets and beams
>   owl and vixen
>   the drub of the sea
>   her voice in sleep
>   by which she tells
>   secrets of loss
>   broken to single
>   syllables
>   to moments of
>   passion or pain

*

Seabirds diving for fish: a wheel of birds ...I saw her shudder.
They found the updraught as one.
They stooped and banked. For a moment, they circled the sun.

As if her look could reach them. As if
she could have that rise-and-stall-and-deadfall-drop
for herself, death drench, ears stopped,
mouth stopped, the shoal rising towards her.

*

> I took her dress
> a perfect fit
> wet from the sea
> still slick with weed
> and while she slept
> (eyes almost closed)
> I hid it then
> turning away
> forgot the place
> as if somehow
> I knew I should.
>
> It's always night
> in this room
> a bloom on mirrors
> salt moon shedding
> a fell dead light

*

She would sense a storm long before it broke:
some shift in the wind or a feathering on the sea,
then the first high gust riddling the trees, first flush
of raindrops creasing the glass, a livid light,
clouds belly-down on the skyline and sudden long lines of rain
beating against the house, so hard and heavy
that everything was water and the sound of water...
She went out. She walked in walking rain.

She might have been naked, the rain
clothed her: I couldn't tell.
She might have been wearing the dress.

                *

                Behind my eyes
                a view of her
                walking through
                gorse and stone
                to dance again
                at the sea's edge
                as she goes in
                soundless and sleek
                my darker shadow
                falls on hers

        *

I let go seven tears into the sea …I netted birds
and broke them open …I walked the pentagram …I set out
water and bread and salt …I laid a track of white pebbles …I burned
myrtle and hyssop …I called the quarters …I cast cards …
I lay a long time in my sweat …it is always night in this room …

Christine McNeill

Kindertotenlieder

The German poet Friedrich Rückert (1788-1866) wrote 428 poems between 1833-34 in response to the death of his two children by scarlet fever, which he called *Kindertotenlieder*. Originally not intended for publication, they were published posthumously in 1872.

Karen Painter in her book *Mahler and his world* (2002) describes the poems thus: 'Rückert's 428 poems on the death of his children became singular, almost manic documents of the psychological endeavour to cope with such loss. In ever new variations Rückert's poems attempt a poetic resuscitation of the children that is punctuated by anguished outbursts. But above all the poems show a quiet acquiescence to fate and to a peaceful world of solace.'

Gustav Mahler chose five of Rückert's poems to set as *Lieder*, which he composed between 1901 and 1904. He picked out the ones that focus on the theme of 'light', indicating that it was important to him to include an element of transcendence. Of Rückert's *Kindertotenlieder* only 36 deal with this theme, and Mahler reshaped them to suit his own purpose. Although it is not known in which order they were written, the first three were composed in 1901, when Mahler was yet to meet Alma, who became his wife. His first daughter, Maria Anna, was born in 1902. A second daughter followed two years later. It was the last two *Kindertotenlieder*, composed in 1904, that alarmed Alma, who described her feelings in her memoirs:

> I found this incomprehensible. I could understand setting such frightful words to music if one had no children, or had lost those one had ... Rückert did not write those harrowing elegies solely out of his imagination; they were dictated by the cruellest loss of his whole life. What I could not understand was bewailing the deaths of children who were in the best of health and spirits ... hardly one hour after having kissed and fondled them. I exclaimed at the time: 'For Heaven's sake, don't tempt Providence.'

Alma's fears turned into reality when in 1907 their first-born daughter Maria Anna died of scarlet fever. On the day of her death Mahler himself was diagnosed with a fatal heart disease of which he died three years later at the age of 50.

Mahler had seen death around him throughout his life: out of fourteen siblings eight brothers and one sister died – five of them in early childhood, the sister died in 1889 aged 26, the same year as Mahler's parents, and his brother Otto committed suicide in 1895 at the age of twenty-two. Then there was his brother Ernst who died at fourteen, who shared the same name as Rückert's son – a loss that affected Mahler deeply, and may have enabled him to identify with a parent's bereavement.

Mahler wrote to Guido Adler about the composition: 'I placed myself in the situation that a child of mine had died. When I really lost my daughter, I could not have written these songs any more.'

Having witnessed so many tragic deaths in his family, it is not surprising that his psyche was drawn to this material. Indeed, before writing the last two songs of *Kindertotenlieder*, Mahler worked on his 6th Symphony, called the 'Tragic'. He himself had had a near-death experience in 1901, when a haemorrhoidal abscess in his abdomen caused him to collapse. During a prolonged convalescence, his thoughts inevitably turned to his mortality.

The *Kindertotenlieder* were written in Mahler's late-romantic idiom, and reflect anguish, the fantasised resuscitation of the children, and resignation. The final song ends in a major key and a mood of transcendence.

It is this element of transcendence that attracts me to Mahler's music. *Kindertotenlieder*, which can either be sung by a baritone or mezzo-soprano, convey moods of longing, of remembrance, dreaming, a world that becomes fluid, where the distinction between 'outer' and 'inner' evaporates – and as such it resembles a child's or the soul's yearning for a lost paradise.

In Rückert's poems there is the interplay of 'dark' and 'light'; the first lines in the first poem say:

> Now the sun wants to
> rise as brightly
> as if nothing terrible had
> happened during the
> night.
> The misfortune had
> happened only to me,
> but the sun shines
> equally on everyone.

The second verse continues with:

> You must not enfold the
> night in you.
> You must sink it in eternal light.
> A little star went out in
> my tent!
> Greetings to the joyful light of the world.

The last sentence betrays a bitter irony.

The idea that Fate is stronger and will overpower one's good intentions pervades these poems.

But finally, when Fate has won – lines in the 5th poem read:

they *(the children)* rest as if in their
mother's house:
frightened by no storm,
sheltered by the Hand of
God.

– an acceptance, or resignation has taken place, and Mahler, in his score, makes it transcend – those children now rest in God.

In my own versions of *Kindertotenlieder* I did not adhere to the original text, instead, my poems came about from intently listening to Mahler's music and to the performance of the vocal soloist. I allowed my imagination to go with what the individual songs and words suggested to me, and the result is something far removed from Rückert's poems.

I wanted to create an ambivalence so that it isn't clear whether the speaker in each poem is the same throughout, or whether each poem focuses on a different bereaved parent, or perhaps on a parent at a different stage of grieving.

At the same time I wanted to stay true to Mahler's mood of remembrance, of longing and dreaming, of a sense of foreboding, the coping with actual loss, and the moving on at the end to something new and unknown.

In his orchestration, Mahler changes the texture from song to song; sometimes strings are used, sometimes woodwind. Only in the final song the two are used together. By this alternation Mahler varied the colouration in a cycle that does not show much movement in key. It starts in D minor, moves to E flat major, and ends in D major. He did this to convey the listlessness of the grief-stricken parent.

Song 1 oscillates between grief and consolation. Unusually, the death knell is played by a glockenspiel, symbol of eternity, and in song 5 it signals the triumph of light over darkness. The ambiguity of song 1 – i.e. that the sun rises regardless of the tragedy that happened at night; that misfortune has befallen the parent, yet the sun shines equally on everyone – portrays a tension that is only resolved in the final song. Mahler greatly intensified the original Rückert poem (song 5). He was aware that for the parent's grief to become transformed, it had to pass through a psychological storm, which the strings convey in this section as a heavy downpour.

For me, listening to the interconnection of orchestration and singer evoked feelings and contemporary settings, which I then tried to explore in my own words.

The version that in some ways connects to Rückert's original is my third poem with its ghost-like remembrance of a lost child. Rückert lost a boy and a girl, and in this third poem, selected by Mahler, refers specifically to the loss of his daughter, and as we now know Mahler a few years after setting the poem to music lost his own daughter. I myself have not lost a child, but, as in Mahler's words, could enter such a situation in my imagination and draw on a reservoir of loss in my psyche.

As a deeply mystical man, yet not conventionally religious, Mahler believed in eternal renewal, as we can see at the end of the song-cycle – a vision which helped him to bear human suffering.

Painter, Karen, *Mahler and his world*. Princeton University Press, 2002.
The German lyrics by Rückert as translated by Emily Ezust.
Friedfeld, Mitch, *Mahler*, 2001.
Mahler-Werfel, Alma, *My life*, 1963.

Kindertotenlieder

(after Mahler)

i

Mother and child

The things I bought at *Mother and Child*
I've chucked into black bags.
All day I cry. Tear up the books
on how to get better.

Not long ago, trees swayed in the wind
when I pushed and screamed
and the future came.
I thought: it could kill me, this child

who wants my milk.
I stroked its soft cheek;
it found my nipple.
It sucked me in.

I light candle after candle.
Stare at the dripping wax.
Snatch an insect off my leg;
watch it wriggle, until dead.

ii

Madness

I pressed the glass so hard,
it cracked in my hand and I bled.
I slashed the bed with a knife,
tore clothes from the wardrobe
and ripped them up.
I made silent phone calls,
stalked young mothers with children,
wishing them dead.
I made cups of tea the way I'd always done,
stirring the sugar in clockwise
for the other way would bring bad luck.
I accused spiders and beetles,
that woman cleaning her window.
I asked for forgiveness;
stared at a crimson rose.

iii

Spooning the past

Taking the spoon
I look at the food
before putting it
in my mouth;

and when I've licked the spoon
I hold it like an open book
or something I've worn for years -
the reflections of my nose, my lips

abandoned and retrieved
as I turn the spoon.
I smile:
as though I've seen

a little face
come in behind; as if each step
creates another
somewhere in the room.

When I put down the spoon,
I gaze into the mirror
at an open door
and feel the air tingle

as if a tiny hand
were brushing against my face;
each step, invisible, unheard,
but in my memory a birth.

iv

Through Water

The day I bought him new shoes
the sun shone and wispy clouds
idled in the sky.

He tried on trainers, strutted up
and down, jumped and hopped,
almost willing the toes to break out.

On and on he walked into the fierce sun,
joining others,
exploring new ground.

A movement, like a fish's fin,
eased down my left cheek,
stopped by the corner of my mouth:

a tear, like a failed adventure.
It's very hot today, the sales assistant said,
handing me water.

I took the half-filled glass,
fearing to drink, as though it were
a deep pool, and I would drown.

V

Moving on

The bunk bed was taken apart.
Next, the desk. One drawer handle
turned up, as if a secret inside
were having a laugh.

The bedside lamp with its yellow shade:
switched on, it glowed like a prayer.

The toys: each one a bell ringing for celebration,
bringing back the moments of playing.

The chair in the corner cried out for its teddy.
A crack in the door-frame where a ball
had been kicked –

and yet the room was so stubbornly at peace.

The bed's angle, dirty socks underneath –
I fixed these random sights into a wordless order,
left a white feather lying.

vi

On a bridge

(After Mahler's Song: 'I have lost track of the world')

Melt-water surges underneath
and in remembered words
I see a bird of prey
carry my loss
into the hairnet of mountain peaks.

Who knows whether we haven't already
been banished into another time?
And the beauty we see – seraphic blue
of a jay
before it slips into the traceries of branches –

is but a small funeral.
I lean into the sight of water surging.
A bird of prey, a moth.
The one has taken off,
the other feeds on the glow of a lamp.

What if I turned off my inner lamp?
Gazed at the spot from which the moth
has flown? Into that small inner glow

casting a warmth on something that was.

Gustav Mahler on the Rax

*'To be out of Vienna, to breathe the clear
fresh mountain air ...'*

Where chamois dice with death in the sun;
where gentians point to the sky's good works;
where an eagle gliding over the valley
holds the secret of love;
and children aren't lost or dead,
but part of the ache:
standing by the cross on the summit
looking down
on hills, fields, woods –
that *ewig, ewig*: the song of the earth.

Jill Townsend

The Auditorium

(Glyndebourne)

The warm belly of its instrument
fills with music frivolous as bubbles
or dark with the melancholy
of double-dealing, strained love.
Indulge these feelings then.

The hours and arias soften
into knowledge, or sleep.
The guilt shared by so many
rests elsewhere as the soprano drops
on to the heart of the financier.

When he lets her go, no doubt
he thinks it's with a kiss. Alone
there's time for reflection
as the night puts on its overcoat
and the stars come out.

King Philip's Aria

(from Don Carlos*)*

His portrait chills —
a cold man with few ideas
beyond the flame of power
buttressed by religion.

But Verdi tells his loneliness,
married to his son's betrothed –
a dutiful wife, just
waiting for heaven.

Eleanor Hooker

Doppelgänger

When did she come in search of me? No, I cannot say
Either. Out of the sea and into the air, forever
Marked by dusk, she is nourished by under-earth
Fusty decay. Blue in summer, green eyed in winter,
I don't believe she has screeched in any of our collaborations.
Yet it's others she favours with ancient eucalyptus,
With willow myrtles. I am her pupil too,
And would love her more than she needs me to hate her.
In deadly night she gives me *Atropa Belladonna,*
Dilates my pupils so wide that the light in everything
Is expressed and swallowed and expressed.
She hums Prokofiev, while I try to discover
The words for her song in my own slurred voice.

Nancy Anne Miller

Falling in Love with a Lake

No waves peak like violin bows,
stretch the crescendo of the tide
up in a careful orchestrated sound
which reaches you at your feet.

This is a flat tune, no rhyming repeats,
just stillness occasionally moved by
the brashness of a fast boat, propeller
causing rivulets, like fans on a hot day

on your island or the hood guy speeding
by your house to impress no one.
The lake a space where a human
swimming makes a ripple, doesn't

mould you chapter by chapter into
its drama like the ocean's push,
pull. As you swim the glassy light,
it holds you up on a silver platter.

John Greening

All I can remember of Neuschwanstein

is that I left my hat inside and had
to tap on the door and ask to be led
back through the dream labyrinth
like following a score to that first E-flat
low horn at the bottom of the Rhine –

and there it hangs, like the last golden
apple of my youth, a chance to escape
the fires, the ring, retirement's rainbow
bridge, the tricks of Loge, Brünnhilde,
Fricka, the whole *Götterdämmerung*.

Turkish Patrol

At the piano, Cypris has taught herself to play
the rondo finale, forgetting what first brought her there.
The crescent moon is giving birth to demi-semi-gods.
The minaret howls an aria from *Il Seraglio*.

Andrew McCulloch

La Scala, 1946

For my father

Rodolfo sings,
   the night is sweet.
Puccini brings
   them to their feet.
Their hearts have wings
   and miss a beat.

The maestro turns,
   takes the applause.
Though music burns
   in all our wars
each new age learns
   to keep its laws.

For pity's sake
   the audience stand.
The poets make
   their old demand
and reach – and take –
   each tiny hand.

Hopkins' Mother

Were his first poems
heartsongs hers
had taught him,
nestled together
in a world-stopping
closeness of blood?

Was this her faith,
her only mortal cure –
his songs, her love –
the rest an envious
male translation,
impossible to believe?

So when he was gripped
by God and knew
it was too deep
for song, who was she to blame –
God, her son, herself –
or her songs?

And was it worse
when the songs came back –
touched by
anothert heart –
screaming now with
Mary's pain?

Armand Silvestre

Two poems

The Secret

Set to music by Fauré

O may the morn never know it,
the name that I spoke to the night:
may it vanish mute as a tear-drop
on the breeze of the early light.

O may the noonday proclaim it,
the love that I hid from the morn:
may it light on my heart, laid open;
may my heart like an incense burn.

may dusk forget my secret,
forget what I told to the day:
in its robe's pale folds may it carry
my love and my secret away.

Translated by **Timothy Adès**

Testament

For the wind to bring you
On remorse's black wing,
On the dead leaf I'll write
My dead heart's suffering.

My sap is all withered
In your beauty's bright noon:
Like the leaf that is faded
My life is all gone.

Cruel suns are your eyes,
To my soul I am burned:
A leaf to the chasm,
Borne off by south wind.

This, first, it shall bring you
On remorse's black wing:
On the dead leaf I'll write
My dead heart's suffering.

Translated by **Timothy Adès**

Giambattista Marino

'Battus!' Ergastus Cried

'Battus!' Ergastus cried: 'This is the hollow
where the fair Chloris chased the fleeing doe,
and fled her chasing swain: nor do I know
if she strove more to flee, or more to follow.

'Look!' he exclaimed. 'You take such joy in hunting
the flitting hart: you shoot it as you please:
then shoot my heart! It bears its wounds in peace,
even pursues you, careless of the wounding.

'You do not hear me out!' Dry-lipped and shaking,
here he fell down, and lay, no longer speaking.
She, cruel, briefly turned on him her eyes.

Love with new searing flames set him alight.
A humour spills from two eyes burning bright:
a humour, which is fire, as none denies.

Translated by **Timothy Adès**

R.V. Bailey

Piano

Like having a piano in the house
We all need someone on whom to practise
Love. Arpeggios of passion, chords of content,
Persistent scales of care, with sharps or flats.

Not necessarily the great concerto
Of long-established wedded partnership –
Short practice pieces, over telephones,
To solitary friends; quick suburban trills
In shopping mall or high street;
Cadenzas in airmail envelopes
For dears Down Under.

But practise, practise. That's the thing
Beethoven sonatas can't be achieved
In a week. Unpractised fingers of love
Won't be sure or supple enough
When there's urgent need for a concert performance
For child, father, friend, neighbour,
Stranger, enemy.

Anne Connolly

Tonic solfa

She practises each day
the doh-ray-me
of public health
major and minor,
never a bumptious note
to echo round the halls
of sterilized bureaucracy.

Warm hands span the tones
of ordinary life,
a vibrant soul, no strings
unless a patient plays her
totally off-key.

She never thinks of Nightingale
as the rat-tat-tat
of repeat prescriptions
reloads the morning,
haemorrhages out
the urgency of coughs and colds
and contraception.

Wan faces line up for immunity
against late-holiday-dot-com
while parents wade their way
through headlines that provoke
a cluster-bomb of indecision.

She hears the febrile murmurs
of a heart that used to sing,
binds up the wounds
which cannot be recorded,
audited and priced
on coalition scales.
So-lah-tea. No time for it.
And far too little dough.

Sarah Wardle

Concert for Anarchy

(after Rebecca Horn)

A grand piano suspended from the ceiling
at intervals performs a high wire act,
upside-down like a girl's hair hanging
as the swing she is on reaches a crest.

So the lid crashes open and the keys
shoot forth in accompaniment,
with a crescendo of disharmony
in a jangling, discordant movement.

Then the piano calmly reassembles
to repeat its explosive piece,
wresting expression and control
from the romantic composer's genius.

Now imagine an entire orchestra
striking in an empty concert hall,
each instrument starring as its own player
and collective conductor of them all,

the bass jazz of cellos and trombones
in counterpoint to flutes and violins,
ticket office photocopier and telephones,
bar bottles and spotlights joining in.

Hope

(after George Frederic Watts)

Who did this to you, blindfolded your beauty,
left you alone on a spinning world,
with no one to listen to your music,
a muse with a broken heart and lyre?
Is this what Zeus did after he had used you,
changed you by metamorphosis
from cheerleader to singer of the blues,
from freethinker to imprisoned pessimist?
Who said you were not good enough for him,
not pretty, young, intelligent and slim?
What man did this, stealing your self-belief?
Or is the truth you did this to yourself?
Your hands are untied. Let in the light!
No more melancholy. Sing of life!

Ann Joyce Mannion

Turnings

for Paul Bewick

What is time now but wind
whipped across island fields or stones
slipping from the order of walls.

He walks boundaries: straight lines
and squared off corners, knows
that everything is not that simple or regular.

An image rolls before him – a woman strolling
down the path eating half-ripened berries
auburn hair burnished in evening light.

Her voice rustles distant trees.
He is bewitched again by the singing
as if it had never stopped.

A cleft of notes resound across the island,
corncrakes rattle love messages to each other
and he is aware of this rooted habit of love

so difficult to let go.
He watches the ebb and flow of the tide,
how it swells the foreshore and eases away.

And it is as though it had never been, all signs lost
save for that ache within, an indelible mark
that stings unexpectedly as he reaches an open gap.

A shoreline has its pocketbook open.
The waterwheel of ocean calls out
the scattered names he has for absence.

Simon Jenner

Handel in the Arcadian Academy

Last year, lusts were proper, my lines all wild.
This academy tries me in Theocritus.
All's balanced with Virgil –
pastoral hesitates across an echo:
equal male and castrati. Damned Pope,
banishing last season's women to be scaled

by Venice or Naples. Rome's cardinal lust
is a state for old men. I'm twenty three,
but to their brown eyes a boy. Above
me are none.

Ottobone, Pamphili, the shepherd
princes pursue me; I notate
their gold-dropped pleasures in *Hendel,
non puo mia misa.*
It's the castrati
nymphs
I give to Pasquinini.

So Pamphili can adore me through Ovid –
His Orpheus forswearing women for peachy boys,
volumined in his rose silk pounce.
Panalphili trialled it in *Trionfo
e del Distuango* – me as *Un leggiadro
giovinetto,* he flutes off in Neapolitan sixths.

He's even Polyphemus lusting for Acis –
I'll set him again back with Galatea
in another country. Rumpy Rumpoli
made his women wail, abandoned to dissonance.
I crushed chromatic grapes to their white skins,
Ariadne to Hero plunged to taste salt.
Rumpoli twitted me as Amintas, had me breathe
my own Phyllis to him. But he lists
for Phyllis in soprano flesh. Trusts
I share his shiver of a joke.

Stuart Medland

Bert's Avocet

(for Bert Jansch, in memorium)

I see your fingers, still, like
wader-stilted legs to
hold a chord of strings,

The other set now
sweeping, upturned, through them,
sieving notes of maverick

Music, just like
water through that
unexpected beak.

In memory of Bert Jansch, the legendary folk guitarist and singer whom I saw play just the once but whose instrumental album Avocet – *a collaboration with Danny Thompson and Martin Jenkins from 1978 – has become part of the soundtrack of my life.*

Willow Warbler

(for John Clare)

In the willow or the birch,
there is the sweet dis-
integration of a song, a

simple tune, undone, a
softly-punctured rush of one

which draws itself up to its
full height and begins again

because there is no more to say –

No more that may be done.

Reedling Music

(to a flock of bearded tits)

Some conductor holds – the bird is barely

An arm's length away and
I have caught my breath while like a
felt-pad piano hammer he begins to
jump the reed with
octave hand-spans –
this way, that.

I have the *sense* of music,
Only – from behind us,
somewhere in the reeds;

Nearly-notes upon the
brink of telling and still
teetering upon their staves – the
hint of a taste of a whisper of a
plainsong trail gone cold of

Shuffling chimes and
watery bells, of dampened
finger-cymbals, fingertips
upon the wine-glass rim, the
topmost nasal chinks of a piano,

Harmonic
tingles on a
string, the

*Ghost of the
vaguest idea for a
wind-in-the-reeds
orchestration.*

I have a sense of more than music;

Cries and wistful counter-cries
for something … always …

Almost lost.

Dan MacIsaac

Northern Shrike

Lanius execubitor

Grey impaler
fills its larder
with locusts and voles
deep in the thornbush;
and along the barbed
twist of the meadow fence
gapes the rictus
of a whitethroat.

Two-ounce killer,
elfin butcher
with tiny cleaver
and lethal hook
kills cleanly
in mid-air
or pierces messily
on littered ground.

Deadly mimic,
the surgical steel
of its voice rings
both false and true
across the raw field,
capturing each
pure pewter note
of its duped prey.

Red Pileated Woodpecker

Dryocopus pileatus

Punk bird,
mohawked,

with a buzzsaw
guffaw,

flaps over
the mosh pit

of glade
to batter

the drumkit
of trunk.

Headbanger bashing
into deadwood,

its blind rage
aimed at

those freakishly
meek grubs

burrowing away
from mayhem.

Norman Buller

Last Songs

(after Richard Strauss)

Tubes of vertical melody
line the walls.
Poems weave
their needles and threads
through music.

The soprano
hovers among words
like a moth.
Song is a silken boat
sailing on silver.

Trees and skies
grope through mists of war.
A garden mourns in rain;
the rose closes its eyes.
This could be death.

Warren Stutely

wight beach winter

a soak of morning
voice all playne shallow

of salt polyphony

chalk a cubist knowledge
of first born

fish syllables

sky wishing young atonals
crystal white

as book craft
ars nova gospels

to the white mouth of o

a water jar of salt blow birds
vowel simplicities

fathom silver
as root wash and glisten

beach cubist

foam and grey charcoal
the consequence of morning

glass ink and glisten
stone grey flute calligraphy

groyne archaic syllable and volume
flight of fish

tangle in quick braque jug
vocabulary

a cut of viols tilt voice bone
stitched in a tan of script

angle a cubist habit of language
strict as parchment

glass early apollo verticles
shell

wash
giotto form as polyvocal white

fresco air
choir blocks of brush tip

craft light vowels sluice
linen speech

moment and blow wave voyager
blue liquid gesture world

David Pollard

Self-Portrait

Maestro Mateo (c1100 - c1200)

*[Sculpture, Portico de la Gloria, The Cathedral
of Santiago de Compostela, Spain]*

Minstrel of hammers exiled from my own creation,
I set myself to kneel eternally in prayer
becalmed behind closed lids,
just here, among the guttering incense
facing the body of James,
apostle of my devotions
       (knowing that, once they had my money in the chests,
       the false friars' would leave their masses)
carved as the curly headed angel of my hopes,
done like the rest in granite
to a black sheen of each one's humours.

To hear their music
      (I mean the angels')
was my passion always.
      (I played the harp and laude
      until the constant dust
      burnt off my fingers from
      the delicate magic of their
      strings and intervals)
that stays much as I always knew it
choral and organo to my dead ears
in stone.

I gave my lintel angels
each an instrument to touch into the air
in brittle silence,
cold above the arches;

made the kings, apostles and the rest
        fratres domini
   (as I)
tilt their ingenious heads
     – so each could show his story,
        knowing my text –
better to hear their music of the spheres.

So my great portico
of the earth's powers
rises from out the stem of Jesse
into glory and the hierarchies of heaven
       (rendered for Don Ferdinando's coin)
sweated through the heat of many summers'
inspiration of the chisel's claw and smoke
into its many mineral skins
I left behind orphaned from me
in their eternal lives.

Lawrence Wilson

modus operandi

eternal question: revelation – how
to say it, how to share the moment of
enlightenment (to use a loaded term)
when perfect words descend like deities
and drop with flawless grace into the waltz
of rhyme and rhythm in the waiting ink?

results are one thing. What you're reading now
is distanced from the lovely torment of
the ringing, rousing moment when the germ
of an idea takes on flesh and flies
like Icarus (but wearing sunscreen), false-
ness burned away, revealing candour. Think

of sculpture, thinking of opera, think of dance:
the years of groundwork, then the blaze of chance

Ride North

David Harsent

Words for Music

On those occasions when I've given a talk on the subject of writing words for music, I often start by pointing out that few people refer to Da Ponte's *Don Giovanni*. Having asserted the superincumbency of music in the undertaking, I might then go on to quote what was said to me by a poet when I was teaching at the Opera Lab: How could a composer set my poem when I've already set it? That first statement and that (yes, rhetorical and challenging) question describe the apparent conflict in the collaboration between composer and librettist. On the one hand, opera is, first and foremost, about music; on the other, whether or not the libretto, or text, is written in verse, it will have its own discrete and intended rhythms. A short lyric set tunefully might more or less hold to the rhythm, the line breaks and the narrative impulse the poet intended; 'Ae Fond Kiss', for example, or 'Drink to Me Only...' Indeed, Burns often wrote with music in mind; it's difficult to think of some of his lyrics – and of Johnson's poem – divorced from their setting. Rossetti's 'In the Bleak Midwinter' is another example.

There's a difference, of course, between words that have been set and those written to accommodate the music, or, perhaps, written at the same time as the music, a symbiosis in which the term 'composition' refers to one act involving both constituents ...which is why I'm so bored by those excruciating debates in which a case is made (or disputed) for the legitimate claim of song lyrics to stand as poetry: the vapid Dylan vs. Keats argument. If the words to a popular song can be comfortably divorced from their music, they won't have been doing their job properly; in fact, I can't, offhand, think of any that might stand alone, not least because once the words have been set, music always has the upper hand. Try reciting the words of any popular song without hearing the music, without feeling pushed into song; it can't be done. A great song will have found a perfect marriage of words and music. The examples are many, so one will do: 'Summertime'. When lyricist and composer are the same, or when lyricist and composer work in harness, then lyric and music are part of a single (if shared) creative drive. The movement of the music will have roughly the same pace as that of the lyric: a sort of hand-over-hand progression, and the two will be properly interdependent. So why that lyric should be torn bleeding and screaming from its music and be told to *Go and stand over there with the poetry* is beyond me.

Two significant compositional differences between song lyrics and libretti (or words written for concert performance, say) stand as evidence of this. They involve rhyme and scansion. It might be that a librettist will use rhyme, but it's fairly certain that his composer won't feel under any obligation to register it, or make it evident. On the other hand, a composer devising music for a pop song, or, perhaps, devising a lyric for an existing tune (much the easier task of the two) will often assist rhyme, or will trade off it. The fact that a high number of popular songs use monorhyme indicates that that insistence tends to work for and with the music. 'Yesterday' is a good example. In fact, McCartney had the tune for the song before he had the words and used filler lyrics (it opened with 'Scrambled eggs') to develop the musical theme, but even the 'as if' lines he devised prefigured the eventual syllable-count and the insistent rhyming: 'Scrambled eggs / Oh, my baby how I love your legs' – which, I confess, are the words that now first come to mind when I hear the tune. The best example I know of monorhyme working with and for the music is the Trolley Song coda from the movie *Meet Me in St. Louis:*

As he started to leave I took hold of his sleeve with my hand / And as if it were planned / He stayed on with me / And it was grand just to stand with his hand holding mine / To the end of the line.

Cleverly integrated, almost punctuative internal- and connective end-rhyme, plus the correct use of the subjunctive. They don't write 'em like that any more.

In modern music (classical – so-called, but used here for purposes of definition) few words, whether lyrics or not, are set tunefully. However, this doesn't mean they were better-treated by the music of the past: an aria from a nineteenth century opera might be tuneful, but it couldn't be read the way it's sung. The same goes for recitative. The music does what it needs to do and if the shape, comprehensibility and stress-pattern of the words has to be compromised, then that will happen; and in fact it always does.

At the world première of *Gawain*, the first full-length opera I wrote with Harrison Birtwistle, I sat next to Michael Tippett. The first act ended with a lengthy masque representing the turning of the seasons: a transitional moment in the poem. In the staging for my version of the Pearl poet's narrative shift, non-singing actors wearing, in their hats, twigs relevant to the season, went clockwise round the stage; someone carried a flag of an appropriate colour: snowy, verdant, etc; Old Father Time went widdershins clad in sackcloth, bearing a scythe and carrying an hourglass. Four seasons, four versions. Twigs and flag changed accordingly; Old Father Time changed, as was proper, not at all. While this was happening, Gawain, attended by members of the court, each singing in turn, and with Bishop Baldwin singing the 'Dies

Irae' *inter alia*, was stripped, washed and armed for his journey. There was, in short, a lot going on.

At the same time, Marie Angel and Elizabeth Laurence, situated in a blue neon hoop up in the flies, sang the turning of the seasons: one lyric soprano, one mezzo. Their joint contribution lasted as long as the onstage events: twenty-five minutes or so. I was reasonably confident that the tenor and baritone voices were rendering my lines comprehensibly; even the countertenor was relatively clear. But as for Morgan Le Fay and Lady de Hautdesert strapped into their hoop and hanging just below the proscenium arch, even I was only getting one word in ten and I'd written it. When the curtain came down, Tippett turned to me as if he had guessed what I was thinking. He said, 'You can never hear the sopranos, dear.' (For 'hear' read 'comprehend'.)

And nor can you. Frankly, you only know what the Queen of the Night is singing if you happen to know what the Queen of the Night is singing. Jeremy Isaacs, who was General Director of the Royal Opera House at the time, had campaigned strongly for sur-titles. There had been an equally strong representation by the producer (opera's term for the director) to do without them. Since the libretto was my copyright, the decision was mine. I consulted the producer, as I felt I should, and was told that sur-titles were 'against the spirit of theatre we were hoping to create'. I had no idea what this meant, but it sounded impressive so I exercised my veto. After the first night I went to Isaacs and gave immediate permission. It might have been – I think it was – the first time a libretto in English was sur-titled to an English-speaking audience. Now sur-titles are almost always used regardless of language and audience. If they're not, it's probably because the performance-space doesn't have the facility.

My position has always been that, somehow or another, my text must be made available to those attending the opera. It might be in the programme, or be handed out as a free pamphlet, or have been published and be on sale; and it will always be sur-titled if I can get my way. This will be the text that is finally arrived at after it has accommodated the composer's needs. There is, of course, a text that precedes the composer's setting, but it's not some sort of Ur-text, a pure vision that was later hopelessly compromised by the composer. Opera is theatre; all theatre is a collaborative undertaking; and since it's most often the composer who will have chosen the subject of the piece, the writer ought to be aware that his collaborator will already have some well-developed ideas of what he's looking for.

In my experience, the collaborative process goes something like this: an agreement between writer and composer on the subject of the piece; an agreement about the approach; composition of text; setting of text. It's during this final process that the initial, and probably most significant, rewrites will occur: the result of an ongoing exchange. Which is as it should be. I was once with Birtwistle in his publisher's office when a pamphlet of my text for *The Corridor*, the short opera we wrote for Aldeburgh, was being desktop-published. Someone called across the office to ask whether the collaboration (I've worked with Birtwistle more often than with any other composer) was usually characterised as 'Words by David Harsent, set to music by Harrison Birtwistle.' Harry called back: 'No, put words by David Harsent, fucked up by Harrison Birtwistle.' Well, yes, it can happen, but not with Harry, whose sensitivity to text is legendary.

Other composers with whom I've worked – Jonathan Dove, Huw Watkins, Alan Lawrence – have shown a similar scrupulousness. After that initial consultation and agreement, I write my libretto. I might – often do – make contact with the composer to ask some question or another and act on the response. Then I deliver the text and the weight of his composition begins to tell on mine. More often than not, this will consist of requests for more text: 'She's on stage, but she's not doing anything.' On one occasion, when he was setting my libretto for *The Minotaur,* Harry called and asked for more lines to be given to Christine Rice (Ariadne) in order to bring a more dramatic and better-integrated end to a scene. 'Make it dark,' he said, 'and not too long.' I wrote an aria: eleven short lines of verse. Had it not been asked for it wouldn't have been there. It is, for me, one of the most compelling moments in the opera. When Christine sang it in rehearsal – not saving her voice – the hairs on my arms lifted and a rill of adrenalin ran on my skin.

At other times, there might be a word that the composer is struggling to set, or it might be that a word is exactly what's lacking. Both Harry Birtwistle and Huw Watkins have asked me to find a substitute for a cry *(Ahhhhhhhh...)* on the grounds that it's a sound in the same way that music is a sound; a word provides an armature. After I handed my libretto for *In the Locked Room* to Huw, I said: 'If you hit a snag, call me.' He called very soon after that and said, 'OK, I've hit a snag.' When I asked him what it was, he said: 'The first word.' Fortunately, the next snag was on page four and the one after that on page eight, and they were all, including the first word, small and manageable. During the composition of *When She Died* – a Channel 4 TV commission that later had a stage production in Vienna – Jonathan Dove identified an entire passage in my text that he couldn't set: an adaptation of a list of healing herbs taken from a book on starcraft and wortconning, a litany of sorts, tightly-cadenced. Jonathan came clean: said something to the effect that it simply didn't serve his purpose – and never would have, I suspect, it being more a case of differing sensibilities than inadvertent redundancy. Given that it is, no question, the job of the librettist to accommodate the composer, I removed the passage and found a different way to progress the scene in question. And

I later used a version of that little incantation in *The Minotaur*.

I was once asked, by an interviewer, who was hoping for a less gnomic response, what I looked for when reading a poem. I said, 'If I can't hear the music, it's not a poem.' (The brevity of my reply was an attempt to supply an honest response while not indulging a banal question with a lengthy answer.) The fact is that, should you allow a poem to be set, *your* music will count for nothing. That's the deal. If you agree to write words the purpose of which is to be set, well, the same applies, but at least you know that and, to some extent, can allow for it. I am, essentially, a narrative poet who trades off of a lyrical vocabulary. In many ways, this suits the demands of opera: my arias have (I think, I hope) some lyric richness while, at the same time, my recit knows how to push the action along, but also has a swing and a lilt to it. The way I approach the task is to write what might, in manuscript, be taken for a stage play. My stage directions will be quite full and the action tend to the episodic (which, were I ever to write a stage play, would almost certainly be my structural method. To a large extent, it's my method in poetry.) I don't necessarily avoid coming at a narrative slant, but I do avoid linguistic complexity: looked at from the composer's point of view, the music is enough to cope with. By and large, though, there isn't a describable technique for writing for music beyond the technique that the writer would consider his own. Perhaps the one thing that should always be borne in mind is that a few words go a long way.

The usual – in my experience the invariable – method in collaboration is that I deliver my text to the composer who sets what I've written apart from those words or passages that cause him problems, or those instances when more libretto is required. There follows a dialogue (not, that is, a series of instructions) about how best to solve those problems. (I say 'invariable' and yoke that term to 'collaboration', because the on the one occasion when my text was radically cut, rewritten and re-structured by a composer, the changes were made without consultation. I found out only when I received the score from the music publisher. This wasn't done because what I'd written wasn't liked, but because the composer simply wanted to make a version of my text that suited his compositional needs and didn't feel the need to make me aware of his intention. My response was to take my name off the piece.

Aside from those precisely concerning text, changes might also be made when issues of stagecraft and narrative progression occur. *Gawain* was twice work-shopped and some re-writing done as a result of that. The same was true of *The Corridor*, when work-shopping the piece brought about a change that not only provoked a radical re-write, but also solved a specific problem in the staging of the piece and, ultimately, had a virtuous effect on its dynamic. It's unlikely, of course, that changes will be made during rehearsals; by then the singers have learned text and music as an indissoluble unit.

The whole business of words that can or can't be set was addressed by Alan Lawrence recently:

> There are words that composers would prefer to avoid; certain obscenities, anything too anatomical, certain place names, supermarket names [1] [...] In general, there seems to be a preference for the rhetorical. Of course one can see that the phonemic structure of this or that word may present a greater or lesser technical difficulty in purely musical terms but one can also wonder whether, at times, the signification of particularly colorful vocabulary is felt to crowd out the possibility of musical setting. The well placed 'cunt', for example, may be considered far too disruptive to the musical thread by reason of invocations unrelated to phonemic or musical structure.
>
> Setting aside such considerations I believe that no word need be unsettable. In instrumental music we find that each instrument has its own range of articulations (accents, stresses, etc.) and timbral variants. Families of instruments and indeed instrumental members of these families vary considerably in the means by which they achieve such inflections but the purpose is the same; i.e. to animate and to characterize the rhythms and pitches of the musical discourse. I find it useful, when considering text for setting, to evaluate words at the level of the phoneme where each element represents an articulation or a timbral variant. (Clearly consonants tend to the articulative and vowels to the timbral.) Considered as such, the text provides an elastic map of articulations and timbral varieties that can be conformed through the imposition of rhythm and pitch (and, of course, accompaniment) to my musical intentions, elucidations or whims. [...] Viewed purely as an indication of sonic potential every word proposes an instance to be accommodated rather than an intrusion to be feared.

That last remark seems crucial, since Lawrence's 'sonic potential' is, I suppose the composer's equivalent of the writer's 'weight' or 'stress'. Not that Lawrence is indifferent to meaning. The text of mine that he set, *The*

---

[1] In fact, I used the name of a supermarket in 'When She Died', which led Mark Lawson, during a feature on *Newsnight Review*, to ask whether the word 'Sainsbury's' was appropriate to opera. Perhaps 'a preference for the rhetorical' is more commonplace than Alan Lawrence suspected, and the commonplace less well approved of; though the key/candle exchange between Mimi and Rudolfo, while not exactly euphuistic, doesn't seem to come in for much criticism on those grounds.

Hoop of the World, is a polemic (though it relies on a folkloric framing device) concerning the near-certainty of eco-disaster, an issue that troubles Lawrence no less than it troubles me – but his stated evaluation of each word is indicative of a care equivalent to that with which the writer, certainly the poet, constructs his (or her) text. Interestingly, although what he says looks democratic, it's not because it can't be; some would say 'shouldn't be' and, frankly, I'd be among them. I ought to say, at once, that Lawrence sees the whole process as a genuine combination of artistic forces and didn't, in fact, ask me for any textual change or modification. Rather, he made the decision to regard the text as immutable, making the point that all composition, whether of words or music, of paint or stone, presents problems which, if not caused by the process of collaboration, will be of the artist's own making; he made the decision to solve both the problems my text raised and those that any compositional act will always involve. So though he's not looking for, not even asking for, superincumbency for his role in things, the fact is he doesn't have to – he already has it because, to put it simply, music is what operas are for.

Which brings me back to the unlikely notion of Da Ponte's *Don Giovanni*. Birtwistle's collaboration, following that with me on *Gawain*, was with Russell Hoban. The opera was *The Second Mrs. Kong*. Hoban came to the general (opera-speak for dress rehearsal) of *Gawain* and seemed, when I met him in the foyer, to be agitated. He was. Apparently, the idea for the piece had been with him for years. I think that, originally, it was going to be a novel. In any event, he had (I'm improvising here) thought about it, dreamed about it, made copious notes on it and sketches for it, developed it and lived it for years before being approached by Harry to work on an opera. Then he'd surrendered it to the project which, even though it was still at a developmental stage, was already being spoken of as *The Second Mrs. Kong: a forthcoming opera by Harrison Birtwistle'*.

Since I'd just been given the news that Marie Angel, who was singing Morgan le Fay, had fainted in a cab on her way to the Opera House, I was a touch distracted and not at all ready for a loaded (and redundant) discussion on ownership, so I simply referred him to the playbill for *Gawain* that was displayed outside and suggested he check whose name was above the title. Of course it's odd and unsettling to have one's project co-opted in that way; it's happened to me when poems I've written – and which preceded any notion of their being set – become the title of a work in another medium by someone other than myself; but since he'd written his text specifically to be set to music, I couldn't quite understand why he was so surprised. It's not that the text is, necessarily, a lesser thing than the music, or of no value without the music (though this can certainly be the case), but it is secondary. And that can, of course, seem unfair, given that it's primary in a temporal sense – here is the poet's subtle and compelling verse-play, a tautly-written and beautifully progressed little psychodrama; and here is the composer to fuck it up. Except of course, crudely put, that's the composer's role.

A final word on words. My involvement in opera came about as much through a love of theatre as a love of music. And though, as I mentioned earlier, aspects of my work for the opera stage would probably be evident in any stage-play I might write, that play wouldn't look anything much like a libretto. On those occasions when I've been commissioned to write poetry for a musical setting, what I write has always worked independently of the music. In fact, I wrote four versions of a song cycle for Birtwistle, three of which he felt he couldn't set. Those three, and the final one, all stand as poems. Conversely, none of my libretti could, I think, be performed by a theatre company.

The difference has to do with precisely the conundrum that was raised at the Opera Lab. The poems have their own music, their own dynamic, their own lodgement, regardless of how music might transform them. And that transformation will only apply in performance. (The exception might be the poem-become-song: Burns, Rossetti.) There's a sense in which, though I might know in advance that the poem will be set to music, I write as if that were not so. It's not that I'm refusing to make concessions; just that this is my setting of my poem and whatever the music does won't change that. A libretto, on the other hand, will change where it must in order to serve the music. But more importantly, and because its declared intention is wholly to accommodate music, the dramatic content of a libretto, the narrative movement no less than the exchanges and monologues, is not so much compromised as good for one purpose only. The opera is not a hybrid form and shouldn't seem to be; it's not the combination of this thing and that thing, but an artistic unity in which both this thing and that thing are crucial and interdependent. The problem is arriving at that unity and in attempting this, the librettist has to understand that the operatic game of give and take is not, and can't be, even-handed.

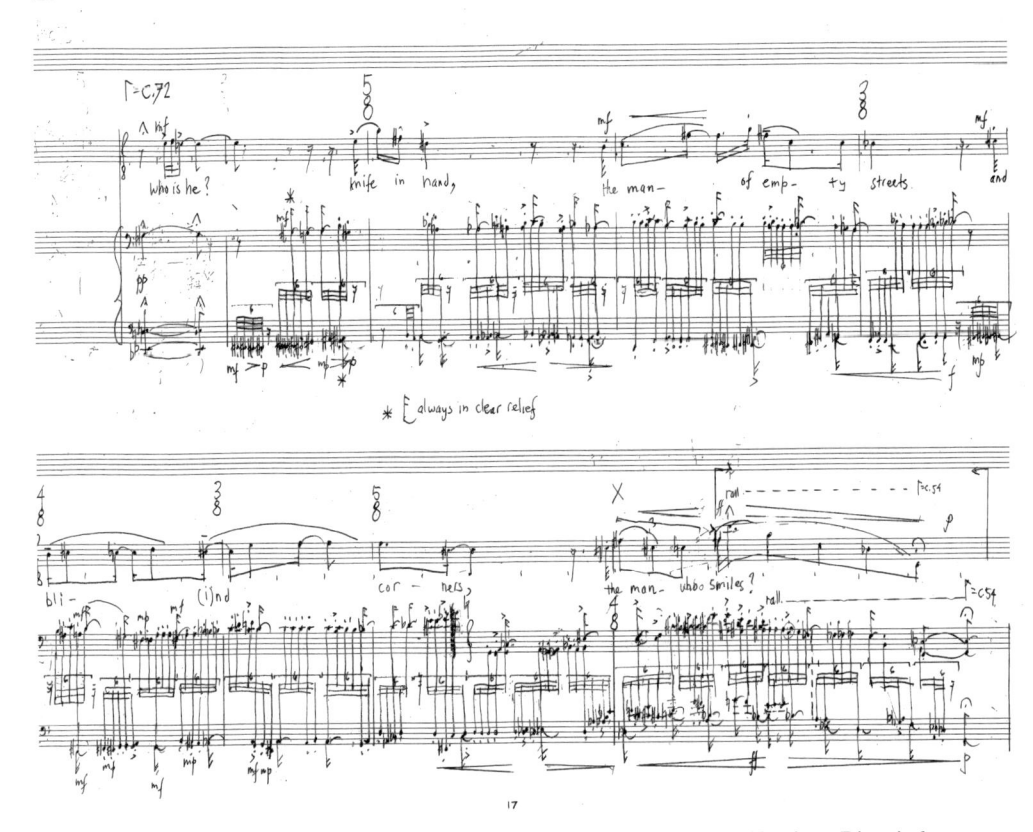

Extract from the score for *Songs from the Same Earth*. Music by Harrison Birtwistle; poems by David Harsent.

© Copyright 2012 by Boosey & Hawkes Music Publishers Ltd
Reproduced by permission of Boosey & Hawkes Music Publishers Ltd

Eric Salzman

Opera, The Writer & The Composer

Opera wasn't always just a composer's art form. The word 'opera' simply means 'work' in Italian. It doesn't make sense as the name for a play set to music unless you realize that the proper term is *'opera lirica'* or 'sung work'. The Florentine intellectuals who invented it called it *dramma per musica, favola in musica* or some such. Their idea was to revive or reinvent what they assumed was the proper performance practice of ancient Greek drama with musical declamation of the text. The main job of the composer (until Monteverdi appeared on the scene, the composers were mostly dilettante singers) was to intone the words to the accompaniment of some chordal strumming, occasionally relieved by a dance tune or two.

Monteverdi proposed a theatrical form that was delicately balanced between music and text and in which music carried the story. After only a generation or two, it evolved into the more familiar sequence of recitatives and arias with all the action and story-telling in the lengthy *recitativo* punctuated by arias expressing the 'affects' – states of mind, emotions, character, vocal charm or just virtuosity. The Monteverdian form survived only in France thanks to a young Florentine composer by the name of Giovanni Battista Lulli; even so, his *tragedies lyriques* (or *tragedies en musique*) were typically billed as works by Philippe Quinault with music by Jean-Baptiste Lully. Back home in Italy, the most famous creator of operas between Monteverdi and the Scarlattis was the poet Pietro Metastasio whose librettos were set over and over again by composers all over Europe. Even Mozart's *Don Giovanni*, dubbed a *dramma giocoso* in Italian, was called a '*singspiel* [or musical play] by Da Ponte' on the original Vienna bill with the composer's name tacked on afterwards. The playbill of *Die Zauberflöte*, a popular musical play if ever there was one, calls it a 'grand opera in two acts by Emanuel Schickaneder'; Mozart's name appears only after the full cast listing. Today, of course, we call them both operas and put the composer's name first.

It took a while for the composers to take charge. Early opera, even when subsidized by the local authorities or nobility, was largely produced by impresarios who hired the talent and had to compete for the biggest singing stars, notably the *castrati* who dominated the *opera seria*. Whereas the early operas and their French successors were mostly based on classical mythology, the 'serious opera' of later times concentrated on the dynastic and love affairs of fabulous pseudo-historical characters portrayed by outlandish superstars wearing extravagant costumes and capable of spectacular vocalism; their efforts were aided and abetted by designers who produced spectacular sets and composers who could supply attractive bare-bones tunes oven-ready for elaborate improvised vocal ornamentation.

Composers began to become international stars in their own right only in the eighteenth century with the successes of the German Hasse *(Il Sassone)* in Italy, the Italian Piccini in France, the German Handel in Italy and Britain, and the Bohemian Gluck in Italy and France. Handel seems to have been the first composer to act as his own impresario. With backing from the fabulously rich English aristocracy, he made regular trips to the Continent to hire the best Italian *virtuosi* (the term meant singers in those days) to come to London; since they were singing in a language that hardly anyone in the public understood, he was able to recycle well-worn Italian material. It was his own personal musical spin and the star casts he put together that made his operas stand out.

As aristocratic support dwindled in the Napoleonic era, theatres and their impresarios had to depend more and more on selling tickets to the bourgeoisie for big spectacles in big houses. Opera houses, stages, orchestras and voices grew in size and, with new lighting technologies (gas and later electricity), theatres became darker, more mysterious, more romantic. Musical scores were now far more extensive, elaborated, more detailed, more specific and more securely locked in, requiring singers to forgo improvisation in favor of volume, projection and breath control. The job of the composer became much more complex and specialized. Responsibility for rehearsing singers as well as orchestra was in the hands of the composer and his music director; there were no stage directors. Verdi and Wagner dominate nineteenth-century opera as no earlier composers ever did.

It is a popular sport to make fun of opera librettos but most Italian and French operas were based on hit plays of the day and occasionally on classics. Texts for singing were put together by professional librettists with little or no input from the original playwrights; entirely original librettos were scarce. The exception was Wagner who solved his libretto problem by writing his own; he ridiculed traditional opera and called his own works 'music dramas'. Ironically, the Wagnerian ideal of music-drama now constitutes the quintessential idea of opera – through-composed costume dramas of substantial length with incomprehensible plots and language, and with large and large-voiced singers who must swim in a sea of orchestral sound. The once-proud intellectual qualities of Wagner's texts, forever debased by the Nazis, and his extravagant use of language and diction are now simply ignored while the composer's domination of the form has become the norm.

The economic as well as the aesthetic model of romantic opera required and continues to require physically large houses, big stages and production apparatus, big orchestras and a big, supported style of vocal projection (amplification is not permitted), all of which makes verbal articulation difficult to impossible, especially in the higher registers. Romantic drama has mostly disappeared in the theatre but it is still the common coin of opera, much as modern directors try to cover it up; neither the theatrical nor the intellectual origins on which the art form was based are much honoured nowadays. Except for Wagner himself, can any reader of these lines name a single librettist between Da Ponte and Boito or Hofmannsthal? Romantic opera survives as a composer's art.

This model still dominates twentieth-century opera even when, as with Debussy and Berg, a playwright's words are set word for word without the intervention of a librettist. Puccini's operas are adapted from plays and through-composed with substantial orchestrations and, as often as not, exotic locations. And, no matter what the subject matter or musical style, modern opera still functions largely within the same nineteenth-century opera-house machinery, a method of bringing dramaturgy to the stage that differs radically from most modern theatre. Even some of the most modernist of operas still depend on post-Wagernian vocalism, large orchestras, opera house performance and opera-house routine, all of which militate for the domination of the musical score (inviolable and untouchable!) and against the comprehensibility of the text.

Several things follow inexorably from this. One is the widespread theory that the sound of the language of the libretto is more important than the meaning of these words. This has led to the relatively recent practice of singing in the original language in all the major opera houses of the world even if, in practice, both sound and meaning are badly mangled by the usual international cast of singers. (This is almost always the case with French and the Slavic languages not to mention the obstacles presented to works that originate in other languages.) Another is the use of titles – used not only for translations from foreign languages but also, amazingly enough, for singing in English! Titles, sur- or otherwise, have the effect of transforming librettos, which used to be a form of dramaturgy, into a print medium.

A third factor is the intervention of the modern stage director with his or her freedom to depart from the original texts (and sub-texts) in ways not available in musical performance. Modernist productions of traditional operas are almost always highly reductionist in their approach to the subject matter. The result of all this is that the actual word-to-word, line-to-line meanings (and, often, rhythms) of the original language are lost on the performers most of whom are, in any case, mouthing languages that they cannot speak or follow. This is bound to affect the way they perform and the way performances are perceived by the public, no matter what the cleverness of the direction or the accuracy of the surtitles.

Is modern opera then inevitably bound to the abstract? Doomed to meaninglessness? Is there anything that can or should be done to rescue the old idea of a words-and-music art form?

In fact, the traditional form survives most obviously in the various kinds of popular musical theatre. Musicals today are also expensive spectacles, often through-composed with substantial orchestration (not always by the composer). However, as with opera when it was still a popular form, they are invariably performed in the local language. Supported singing in the operatic tradition, with its heavy emphasis on vowels and comprehensibility problems in the higher registers, is either not used at all or only in a severely modified form and the voices are boosted by amplification. Supertitles are not used.

These distinctions are significant. Opera is a supported art form with an emphasis on the classics, nearly always performed in quotation marks and appealing primarily to a specialized audience of connoisseurs. The Broadway/West End/Hamburg musical theatre is a popular and direct entertainment aimed at a mass audience that is generally more open to new work of one sort or another! There are obvious issues here of economics as well as of class but I will leave such (currently unfashionable) considerations to others.

If we take a step back, it becomes clear that opera is 'just' a historically and culturally bound form of musical theatre and that its baroque and romantic practices no more define the possibilities of theatre-in-music than any other such form – Chinese opera, say, or the music video. There is an argument to be made that the opera can no longer renew itself out of its baroque/romantic form and that new relationships between the composer and the writer (let alone director, choreographer and designer) cannot come about with the restrictions of the grandiose machinery and physical size of the modern opera house.

Music theatre in the theatre offers other opportunities. It is an odd fact of recent operatic history that virtually all the successful American operas of the past century – from *Four Saints in Three Acts* and *Porgy and Bess* to *Lost in the Stars* and *Sweeney Todd* started life in the theatre.

Although today's 'uptown' musical theatre is expensive and gaudy, there is also the possibility of a small-scale 'downtown' music-theatre theatre – an off-Broadway of opera or opera fringe, if you will, with small casts and simple instrumentation. Amplification might be used (or not) as part of the modern music-theatre took-kit and the range of modern vocal styles are available. Like other kinds of theatre, it would be located in its time and place and would likewise have to engage directly with a public in its own language, whatever that might be.

All this is not just a matter of musical aesthetics. Small is beautiful but it is also practical. There is no reason why a music-driven theatre should be so expensive or so drastically out of reach of its potential public. There is also no reason why sung language in music theatre should not be as comprehensible (or, if required, incomprehensible) as in a pop song or a rap.

The writer's involvement in creating a music-theatre work may involve more than just lyrics to be set to music; depending on the nature of the collaboration, it might include the *mise-en-scène*, the physicality of the performance, the theatrical concept itself. The small theatre situation permits interaction between the creators, between the creators and the performers and, ultimately, between the artists and the public, all in ways that are extremely difficult (not to say impossible) inside the heavy machinery and antique routine of the opera company. The concept of a new music-theatre theatre may even suggest the idea of a lighter but serious music-theatre culture with new works, new kinds of works, new collaborations and new kinds of collaboration. A new *opera seria*? Why not?

Cassandra Ground Zero

Poem/Libretto

Words: Eva Salzman
Music/Score: Eric Salzman
Realised by Kristin Norderval as Cassandra

Performed

Ultima Festival

Oslo, Norway – October 5, 2001
&
New Opera 11
Vienna, Austria – November 2002
&
6-Tage-Oper 2004
Dusseldorf, Germany – February 13, 2004

Extract: last three verses:

Only those about to die,
those at the wrong end of the muzzle of a gun,
in the shadow of the lucky and saved,
are ever called brave.

Only those about to die,
those at the wrong end of a hunting knife,
those halfway out to sea or on the run,
are ever called brave.

Only those about to die,
poised at the edge of a canyon,
at the wrong end of a vengeful sorry life,
are ever called brave.

A Tempo, fast soft-shoe tempo, 2 to the bar
breathy tone; very articulated; like a little dance
C
p
On - ly those a - bout to die, at the wrong end of a gun, in the shad-ow of the
[melange of cicadas, gulls, helicopter, etc]
6
C
luck - y, the saved, are ev - er called brave.
fresh start; stronger
mf
On - ly those a -
sffz
mf
11
bout to die at the wrong end of a knife, half-way out to sea or on the
3
16
run, are ev - er called brave.
f
On - ly those a - bout to die, at the
f

C
hand of a venge - ful wife, poised at the edge of the rift of their sor - ry
sfz
f
life, are ev - er called brave.
I'm so hot!
You're not! Wait and see. It's a ris - ing sea. Be brave. Get this down.
ocean sounds, gulls, cicadas
she goes into the house
Save.
ocean sounds, gulls fade

Michael McCarthy

Poetry and Opera

As a director, commissioner and developer of new opera for over 30 years I have been engaged in the perpetual debate about how to balance words and music in opera, and more specifically about the nature of the words opera needs. With Music Theatre Wales, the company I founded with my colleague and conductor Michael Rafferty reaching its 25th anniversary, this seems a good time to take stock.

First and foremost opera is a dramatic form. It is theatre, but its primary language is music. For opera to work, the music needs to convey the drama in all its aspects – the individual characters and their encounters, the mood of each scene covering not only the attitude and tone of the characters involved but also the atmosphere of the location, the pacing of the drama, and the focus and exploration of the dramatic thrust – in other words, the issues that the drama aims to explore. Perhaps most of all, the music, and therefore the composer, needs to explore the things that are unsaid and often cannot be said, and this is where the discussion of the role of the writer becomes really interesting.

Music has the power to dig deep into the emotional, psychological and imaginative worlds of the characters on stage, and has the ability to operate on a number of different levels at the same time. The orchestral score can depict the surface aspects such as mood, setting and attitude, but it can also suggest things that the characters themselves may not yet be able to articulate, such as intuition and instinct. At the same time, the music can indicate to the audience that something is about to change, at the very moment that the character believes that everything is settled (this is a classic horror movie trick – when the sound track clearly indicates there is something lurking around the corner in order to heighten our senses and the impact of the discovery on the unsuspecting protagonist). But there is another very powerful musical and expressive tool the composer has at hand – the singing! In general we need words to sing, but one of the greatest strengths of opera is the fact that through the way the characters sing we hear much more than the words. If we don't, why bother singing them?

This is the joy and challenge of opera for writers. Opera needs text that articulates the structure of the drama, that depicts character, intention, conflict and progression and which conveys genuine theatrical expression and meaning. Having done all that, the text also needs to enable the music to take narrative and expressive control. It needs to give rise to the musical expression so that the drama itself can take flight and reach into the unspeakable depths we aspire great art to take us to. The text needs to provide structure and content whilst accepting that it is the means through which opera can happen and not the reason for opera to exist.

So where do we find the writers for opera – the librettists?

Do we start with theatrical writers and play texts? Frankly, if a play is working I can't see much point in setting it as an opera unless it is re-imagined and re-structured. Operas are not plays with music. The only point in taking a play as the basis for an opera is because it has strong theatrical qualities and because the composer can hear it in music. The idea or intention of the drama needs to chime with the instincts and desires of the composer, but the language is by definition completely different. It is the same with taking a novel or folk tale. To make any of these source materials into operatic text you have to collect all the material of interest, melt it down and re-cast it in a new form. Of course, some plays and stories will survive more intact than others, but to sing a whole play would not only make for a very long evening (it takes a lot longer to sing something than to speak it), it would deny the very qualities that make it a good play – the way that language itself is used to develop and deliver the drama, and what is required to make a good opera – the musicalisation of the drama.

Opera has a long and successful history of using myths as dramatic source material, and there's good reason for this. Myth works because it deals with the very essence of being alive, of breathing, thinking and feeling. It addresses what it is to be human, often through dramas that stand outside normal everyday life, but nevertheless touch us. I think this is also one of the great strengths of opera and its potential to touch us emotionally and viscerally as well as provoking our thoughts and even changing the way we see the world. But there's no point in just taking a myth and presenting it as an ancient tale. It needs to have something to say to us now. It needs re-vitalising and re-imagining as a new work which is conveyed through a new language, and this needs a writer as much as it needs a composer.

Telling modern stories in opera can be tricky. Opera is not good at kitchen sink drama. Dialogue is a challenge – it's not impossible, but it is very difficult to pull off. If the question 'Why are they singing?' rears its ugly head, then there must be something wrong, and that's usually because it's the wrong text being sung, not the fact that they are singing. As I explain above, singing is a fundamental aspect of the language of opera, a key component. That said, I do think we need modern stories if opera is going to continue to function and find a new audience, so we have to find, or better still create these stories. Again, we need writers for this!

What writers? Who are the opera writers or librettists of the future? Where do we look and who do we talk to?

I think it is a well-worn cliché that poets make librettists. I know that some poets make excellent librettists but others don't. It is also a cliché that all composers can and should write opera. There is abundant evidence to contradict this statement.

Given opera is drama, what we actually need is dramatists – both for the creation of the text and for the composition of the music. Two dramatists might seem excessive, and some argue for the inclusion of a third – the director and even a fourth, the dramaturge, but I think this simply demonstrates the level of complexity in creating new opera. I will put aside the argument for the inclusion of the director in the writing process, because I often think this is used to provide a sticking plaster to cover the fundamental lack of dramatic instinct and knowledge between the writer and composer (and in the UK for the lack of a dramaturge), even though having a theatrical mind can be a great help in some instances.

This is not the space to explore the idea of what a dramatist really is, but suffice to say it is someone who understands how an idea is conveyed through drama and how to theatricalise an idea. They need to know how the theatre works, how to tell stories, how to create and differentiate character, how to control the build and release of tension and intensity, how to structure the drama to maximise its impact. All theatre writers (or dramatists as they are often called) have to think about this, but not necessarily poets. My challenge to budding opera composers is that they also need to think like this. They have to take responsibility for every single aspect of the drama once they start work. They cannot rely on the text to do it for them. If a composer simply follows the text it's not going to work as an opera. In fact, the composer has to take responsibility for the delivery of the text in the same way as the director and actor for a play. In the rehearsal room, the actor and director will work together to establish the tempo, intonation and inflection required to work with the text and within the direction of the particular production. In opera it is the composer who establishes the mood and tempo of each scene and every word, who chooses where to focus and what to explore in the piece. Ultimately, the composer controls the entirety of the drama. The opera director will then come in and react to the entire text they have to work with – in other words the score, not just the libretto. The composer has to think as a dramatist as well as composer, but they can only do this if they are totally in harmony with the text they are working with.

So why are poets so often cited as ideal librettists?

I would suggest this is because opera text requires brevity and depth, because it needs to carry the potential for exploration and development through music, to touch on instincts and emotional impulses, and to provoke and release the imagination. The poet as opera writer seems to evolve from two places: (i) thinking of the ancient Greek dramatists as poets and (ii) the perpetual use of poetry in music as a source of inspiration and for song. That's fine, but the Greeks who wrote the great dramas of the day were of course true dramatists writing in a heightened language that was not related to the everyday but which carried powerful meaning, and poetry itself is not by definition drama.

Brevity of text is essential, but the brevity has to have purpose. It needs to carry what is unsaid as much as what is said. Poets and playwrights understand this, all writers do, but perhaps it is first and foremost the poet's stock-in-trade. Playwrights use text and actors and directors to explore the unsaid, if that's not too much of a contradiction, but composers can plunge into the heart of the unsaid and unsayable without out saying anything (in text).

Poets have much to offer opera, so long as they are also real dramatists and willing collaborators. The collaboration between writer and composer is essential and I think that most of the real work takes place before a note is written. It's not good enough for the composer simply to wait for the text to arrive without being fully immersed in the evolution of the drama, hand-in-hand with the writer. But the letting-go also needs to be understood. The librettist has to accept that the composer needs to take full control, even possession of his/her text. The composer can't do this without the text but he/she needs to work with it and consume it, to expand it and command it whilst also loving and respecting it. And remember this. A libretto is not a complete thing. It exists to be turned into an opera. It is the framework which carries the essence of what is to be said and more importantly what is to be experienced. It is the place from which an opera can start to come to life.

Susan Wicks

Those Live Moments: Thoughts on Poetry and Music

Perhaps the most memorable evocation of music in literature is Swann's first true meeting with 'the little phrase' of Vinteuil's sonata for piano and violin in Proust's *Remembrance of Things Past*. Swann, like many otherwise sensitive and educated people, is musically ignorant, and so in a sense privileged: from his first confused impression comes 'the only purely musical' appreciation – 'limited in [its] extent, entirely original, and irreducible to any other kind.'[1] This activates musical memory and brings real delight. But it is by nature elusive. Swann keeps trying to flesh it out in other terms – it's moonlight on the sea, it expands the lungs like the smell of roses – but it is by nature resistant and transitory. And already it's too late. In spite of himself Swann is hooked, searching, hopelessly torn between the concrete world and the abstract world of memory and imagination. He is 'in love'.

When Patricia McCarthy mentioned she was planning an issue of poems on the subject of music, I was immediately struck by how few of these I've written, whereas all the visual arts and crafts, from painting, sculpture and photography to architecture, ceramics and fabrics, seem a continued inspiration for possible new work. I don't think I'm alone in this: visual representations are more readily evoked in what we like to call 'the mind's eye', yet at the same time cry out for a narrative that will give them an existence in time – and poetry, as Fiona Sampson underlined in her 2011 Newcastle/Bloodaxe *Poetry Lectures*,[2] is an art that unfolds to the ear in time, quite as much as presenting its shape, patterns and claim for special attention to the eye. Most of us surely dream in pictures, narratives, touch and speech, and poetry for me is something multi-layered, which does not exclude that dimension of subliminal response.

Most of the poetry that takes music as its ostensible subject is not in fact about music. It is an invitation to memory, and the memory immediately summons up other senses. In D.H. Lawrence's 'Piano', for instance, the memory is spatial and tactile, as well as auditory:

---

[1] Marcel Proust, *Remembrance of Things Past* (trans. C.K.Scott Moncrieff; Penguin, 1981), vol.I, pp.227-8).
[2] Fiona Sampson, *Music Lessons* (Tarset, ,Bloodaxe, 2011)

A child sitting under the piano, in the boom of the tingling strings
And pressing the small, poised feet of a mother who smiles as she sings.

The diction itself is rarely confined to what can be heard. No sooner do we begin to hear the music than it twists away from us into smell and touch and taste, which, for Philip Levine, is the taste of breath – 'part milk, part iron, part blood, as it passes/ from me into the world.'[3] If music 'remembers better'[4], *what* it remembers tends to be not musical but human, and inextricable, as the human tends to be, from a story of pleasure or pain.

There is a sense, Levine seems to suggest, in which music can come to our aid when the visual world fails us: 'It's what we need/ as the sun staggers behind the low gray clouds/ blowing relentlessly in from that nameless ocean [...]'. And, trawling through poem after musical poem, I was struck by how often the musical subject was introduced by a reference to low light or even darkness. On the one hand, we need, in our poems as in our lives, to block out the visual before we can properly 'hear'; on the other hand, if life happens to rob us of our 'light', it is music that can most readily bring it back.

Now I have a context for my initial surprise. If in my own poems visual impressions predominate and truly musical subjects are infrequent, I'm in extremely good company. Just recently, though, I've been working on an extended piece that's aiming to be more open and comprehensive, and I was half-amused to find that in this piece there are a number of musical references, from the Basque carol, 'Gabriel's Message' and the *Nutcracker*, through *La Bohème* and *Le Nozze di Figaro*, to the James Bond theme – with room, no doubt, for many more! Suddenly they seem to me to be part of the pattern – part of *my* pattern – a pattern that is cultural as well as individual, and open to life's own chaotic juxtapositions – open also to risk, and inviting a real possibility of failure.

Yet some poets do manage to write subtly and memorably about music. Not many as searchingly as Proust does; perhaps we recognize that the poem is already a kind of verbal music and that to put music centre-stage risks making the poem self-conscious and self-referential? Our contemporary orthodoxy in this country is to work in the other direction – from the immediacy of the concrete object or occasion towards a wider or deeper suggested abstract meaning, rather than from the abstract towards an expressive 'bodying forth'.

---

[3] Philip Levine, 'Call It Music', from *Breath* (New York, Knopf, 2004), reprinted in *Stranger to Nothing: Selected Poems* (Bloodaxe, 2006)
[4] Anne Sexton, 'Music Swims Back To Me', from *Selected Poems of Anne Sexton,* ed. Diana Wood Middlebrook and Diana Hume George (New York: First Mariner Books,2000) , p.12.

Even poet-musicians like Caroline Price seem drawn primarily by the first possibility. In 'The Violinist's Granddaughter'[5], a poem about her teaching of Nina Joachim, the pupil's musical aspirations express themselves physically as she measures her own hand, bent and stiffened by arthritis, against the ideal ceramic hand made from a cast of her grandfather's. Yet for the poet the ceramic fingers are themselves in the process of becoming something else, 'all frailties cast out', as the living violinist stands 'hand in hand' with the dead one, 'believing everything is possible'.

This is at the same time a poem about aspiration and a poem about human inadequacy. For me, this is what poetry about music can convey best – not just the beautiful abstraction, but the paradox that is our living, breathing, failing relationship with it. When the American poet Suzanne Cleary writes in a poem called 'Glory'[6] about a scratch performance of Handel's *Messiah* at Carnegie Hall, she writes also about the limits of our knowledge of one another and their sublimation in music, the 'musical' magic of intense listening. Music in poetry is also memory and expectation of music. As Cleary puts it in the final lines of another poem, 'Music for the Desert Island'[7]:

> I would not need one note
> if I could hear those live moments
> when the song had just ended,
> or when it had nearly begun,
> when everyone, everyone listening
> held perfectly still, or failed to.

---

[5] from *Pictures against Skin* (Ware, Rockingham, 1994).
[6] from *Keeping Time* (Pittsburgh, Carnegie Mellon, 2002)
[7] from *Trick Pear* ((Pittsburgh, Carnegie Mellon, 2007)

Thomas Adès

A Path into the Heart: Shakespeare's *The Tempest* translated into Opera

Meredith Oakes and I decided to make an opera on *The Tempest*. The play is a siren song to composers, but as soon as one gets close to it with a view to commuting it into a flowing musical structure, obstacles emerge.

The music of Shakespeare's language sings its own peerless song when spoken well on the stage; but to find the inner music of the drama, as maybe Verdi and Boito did with *Othello* to make *Otello*, required a translation of the original. I was viscerally certain that any form of 'heritage' Shakespeare opera would be a time-wasting horror, and therefore it was crucial to avoid the distraction of chunks of specifically 'historical' language. I didn't want to be like a bad tour guide pointing out a gable here, a mullioned window there, when we are trying to find a path into the heart, into the deeper poetry, the 'music' of the play.

Aware that concern might be felt over the 'loss' of Shakespeare's language – as if by translating the play into an opera, we were erasing every existing copy of the text – I persuaded Meredith to insert one Shakespearean word into the text of the opera, of which the meaning is not certainly known. This word, 'scamels', is used by Caliban, when drunk and ranting about the riches of the Island; scholars cannot determine whether it is a bird or a fish. The court responds: 'What are scamels?'

This is how I imagine the internal reaction of an audience to a *Tempest* opera, line after line, if one had set Shakespeare unadapted. But there is a wider point: the language of the play is magnificently gnarled, the dialogues often repetitive, the characters notoriously ambivalent about motive. These are among its joys; but there is nothing except frustration and redundancy to be gained from them in an operatic setting.

Meredith's linear approach was the key that unlocked for me the garden of *The Tempest*, so that I could breathe its air and hear its colours in my first language – music. I remember telling her during the process of composition how I felt as if the lines were the channel of a canal, down which, when all was well, the music could flow unimpeded. She said: 'When you are making a garden and want a wild, tangled effect, you don't lay down twisting, windy paths; you lay down straight, rectangular paths. It's the plants that make the effect.'

Beginning of Act I, scene III, *The Tempest* by Thomas Adès

N. S. Thompson

Ceyx and Alcyone: Notes for a 'Pocket Opera' in verse

Why should a poet write the text (libretto) for an opera? After all, who would remember his or her words under (as it were) the music? Was it not Rossini who said give me a laundry list and I will set it to music (*'Datemi una lista della lavanderia ed io ve l metterò in musica'*)? What he was saying, in effect, was 'who needs the words?' But it was not always so; the first opera was composed in an equal collaboration between a librettist and a composer, both of whom belonged to the sixteenth century Italian Humanist circle, the Florentine Camerata, that began to discuss the performance of Greek theatre and concluded rightly that it was sung. Why else have a 'khoros' and 'orkestra'? Thus Jacopo Peri (composer) and Ottavio Rinuccini (poet) created *Dafne*, the story of the Greek nymph's transformation into the laurel tree – a favourite Renaissance theme – that was put on in the house of music patron Jacopo Corsi in 1597 or 1598. Its success led other composers to work with Rinuccini and under the patronage of the Medici this new art form flourished, culminating in Monteverdi's *Orfeo* (1607). It was from these modest, if erudite, beginnings, that grand opera began.

But why should a poet write the words? Apart from the very good reason that opera is dealing with a marriage of metrical words and metrical notes, there is another creative reason to consider: artists like to collaborate. What could be more satisfying than taking a part in what has become the most spectacular of all the arts in its combination of music, narrative, theatre, design, and – yes – poetry? The trouble is that quite often the composer has had to make do with a laundry list and, even worse, has been satisfied to work with one. It is true Rinuccini was one of many late Renaissance Petrarchan poets who worked in a careful *ottava rima*, but was able to vary the text by the inclusion of other stanzaic and metrical forms. In his day it was noted that his words were always heard and blended well with the music. How different from the contortions that many nineteenth century Italian composers had to make with their libretti: even Italians can barely grasp what is being said in arpeggiated words and a highly archaic diction not that far removed from the Renaissance.

There is also a second creative and more technical consideration that takes us back to formal stanzas and metrics: the challenge of creating a drama in verse. Modern theatrical taste has lost any liking for it (despite the pioneering efforts of Eliot, Auden and Fry to reintroduce it), which hypothetically leaves the opera, if one could find a willing composer (not to mention an audience).

If one looks at many recent operas, the libretto is in prose. But why does this have to be? At their best, formal metrics guide a poet to concision and this helps him or her to avoid false ornament. As Eliot once said: 'Poetry is not an embellishment, but a medium to look through.'

On the other hand, as Auden has said, 'Opera is the last refuge of the High Style' and this is perhaps why many composers, since Benjamin Britten first made contemporary opera viable again – especially in the Anglo-Saxon world – have followed his example in using celebrated plays or novels as a base text. We can think of a huge range from Carlisle Floyd's opera of John Steinbeck's *Of Mice and Men* to Thomas Adès's recent version of Shakespeare's *Tempest*. There have also been notable successes using contemporary themes, but then John Adams's *Nixon in China* has an incredibly heightened subject matter of enormous historical importance. The contrast between two world leaders and two world systems could not have been greater. Thus the potential for tension, irony and even satire was huge and Alice Goodman wrote an exceptionally evocative libretto. But there have been many more treatments of modern myths and characters that have been enormous flops, and I would posit that the reason for this is the casual manners and contrasting hype of today do not make for emotional heightening.

Thus I was drawn to a classical narrative, agreeing with one critic's view that 'a poignant theme involving symbolic characters within an imaginative atmosphere' enables the portrayal of 'the elemental, emotional realities of life in contradistinction to the socio-economic issues which constitute the realm of naturalistic prose drama.'

I first came to the story of Ceyx and Alcyone in a child's version of selected tales of Ovid and was charmed by the story of these two lovers who become metamorphosed in 'halcyon birds', even though I had no idea what these birds actually were; nor do we still. Later on, I was surprised to find them as the first exemplum in the poignant framework of Chaucer's *The Book of the Duchess*, an exploration of sorrow, loss and bereavement, where the much-truncated narrative serves to introduce the theme. Chaucer cuts the beautiful transformation into birds, but adds something I found irresistible: the touch of comedy. And lastly I came to the source, Ovid's *Metamorphoses*, Book XI, 221-748 ('Namque senex Thetidi…').

The narrative of two tragic lovers metamorphosed by the gods into halcyon birds seemed to me the ideal narrative for a chamber opera (or 'pocket opera' as I prefer to call it): a cast of no more than six (Ceyx doubling as Morpheus, son of the God of Sleep), a chorus of flexible number, but with huge scope for effects and, above all, emotionally engaging music. It was imperative to allow the composer as much scope as possible while maintaining a narrative framework and dictating to some extent the way it should be played dramatically (including suggesting duos and trios). Essentially, the work is to be a collaboration, especially in some key parts.

The work is divided into two acts: the first depends on the interplay of characters and builds to Ceyx's crisis of conscience as he sets sail for the Delphi oracle to find the cause of suffering. The second act is less dependent on words of explanation, more on the forces that move Alcyone. The two parts are separated by the storm in which Ceyx's ship comes to grief. And there are various ways of doing this: you could have the full Shakespearean storm at sea of *Othello* ((followed by Verdi), *Twelfth Night* (in Trevor Nunn's version) or *The Tempest*, or perhaps the inner storm of Ceyx's troubled mind as he wonders why men are so cruel and evil to each other. I have left this scene undeveloped, as with others, preferring to work with the composer here.

Equally suggestive is the scene where the gods' messenger Iris goes to wake Somnus to engage his help in bringing a dream to Alcyone to reveal Ceyx's fate to her, so relieving her suffering and anxiety with tragic certainty. Here I took a cue from Chaucer in having a comic scene where the splendidly iridescent messenger is unable to wake Somnus. She is left on stage humming to herself and I had the idea that this could be a scene with alternating flashing colours and shade and a vast collage of music, sampling popular songs, classic music and electronic effects. Indeed, despite the Classical tale, the score does not have to be for a classical orchestra: electronic instruments and Oriental percussion could perform it and certainly I would not discount the use of modal music and simple pentatonics. Essentially, this lively scene should have all the vibrant sensations of a dream sequence and provide a contrast with the preceding storm scene and the following pathos when Somnus sends his son Morpheus disguised as Ceyx to visit Alcyone in a dream at night and tell her of his fate. These three scenes – storm, Iris in the cave of Somnus, Morpheus's visit – are the dramatic highlights where I hope there would be an intense collaboration with the composer and director in a multi-media collage of sounds and effects (sonic and visual). Indeed, I see the ending, where the gods take pity on the two lovers and transform them into birds, utilising a huge back projection of sea and sky and the flight of two birds, which could use animation rather than actuality, seeing that we have no record of what the Greeks meant by a 'halcyon bird'.

The versification was written to be equally flexible. There are no set stanza forms such as ottava rima, sonnet or villanelle, nor are there (at present) prose passages of recitative. I find recitative breaks the illusion, especially in eighteenth century opera, and believe that if opera is to be opera then as far as possible it should conform to its musical nature. Thus I used a variety of metrical lines from two syllables upwards and hope to have paid attention to how the words would sound as music. Obviously the Greek names are ripe for treatment and could be rendered in such a way where the voice is purely an instrument, as in much nineteenth century opera, where the music often overrides the words. But here the use of pure syllabic sounds would be acceptable.

However, one element I would like to introduce is where a spoken or barely sung word or phrase is used to undercut the music and the emotion and introduce either of those Greek notions of bathos or pathos, and also comedy. For example, Ceyx is explaining his grief to Peleus, how his brother Daedalion challenged the gods for violating his daughter Chione, who bore sons to Apollo (Philammon) and Hermes (Autolycus). In order to express his desperation over the gods' messy love lives and their effect on men, I suggest he gives up on the music and simply bleats the last line:

> All brass and polish till his daughter Chione
> Was courted by Olympians,
> Athletically forceful and in rivalry.
> Eventually she bore them twins:
> Apollo fathered Philammon,
> Hermes Autolycus...
> ....
> ....What a fuss!

The line of suspension dots suggests that there may be a flourish of music here and then the hopelessness and disgust of Ceyx's last phrase. These dramatic effects I think are legitimate for a librettist to offer. If they are not accepted, then that is the nature of artistic collaboration.

Furthermore, in line with a fairly simple narrative, I wanted to keep the diction as simple but as evocative as possible, hoping to use the sound of the words more than intricate word play and erudite associations. This of course contrasts with Ovid, who has splendid descriptions as well, such as the entrance to Somnus's cavern (XI, 592-615), which I could have had Iris sing, likewise the many descriptive locations, but these could easily be suggested by the setting.

A final word on the production, which I felt had to be kept in mind all through the writing: how is this going to look on stage? As a 'pocket opera' (and in the hope of getting it produced, once a composer had agreed to work on it), it could be performed both simply (cheaply) and grandly (expensively). It would not need many props (only the sound of sheep and cattle, not their actual presence, when Peleus arrives), but I did think back projection would be simple and effective for the storm scene and also the ending where Alcyone and Ceyx are turned into halcyons. As mentioned above, this could even be done via animation.

So although an opera libretto may look rather spare, it does come with a lot of thought about the mechanics of creating a drama with music, where the music is the main vehicle for the emotion, and the dramatic production the vehicle for communication with the audience. If this particular libretto looks modest, it is to allow the many other potential collaborators to have a say as well. After all, Ottavio Rinuccini managed with a mere 455 lines and his orchestra consisted simply of harpsichord, lute, viol, archlute and triple flute.

Winter

Sally Long

When Rebecca Sings

When Rebecca sings
her words soar like birds
riding on air currents.

Her notes rise and fall
like waves that ebb and flow
when the moon tugs at them.

She sings with the freedom
of a refreshing wind,
how I envy Rebecca's voice!

Smooth – sleek and rich
as a marten's fur, warming
a shimmer of summer sun.

James Simpson

Wind from the North

ἅπαντα τίκτει χθὼν πάλιν τε λαμβάνει.
        Antiope (Unplaced fragment, line 195)

            i

One hundred and fifty six remain
in the ash of the merchant's house;

some struggle, some seem resigned,
some tuck in their knees

to return to their mother's belly.
We dowse for water waiting

for the hazel twig to twitch,
but there are still eight loaves

cut and ready to be sold;
cracked walnut shells in the tavern fireplace.

            ii

Men with mattocks
are cutting
into the cuckoo hill;
the place they say
befitting of maidens.

Wheatear, wheatear,
            from one tussock to another;
horse smatch, fallow lunch,
            from there to the other.

They are breaking open
the mound
with bare hands,
some with axes;
to find a child woven,
swaddled and swollen.

Wheatear, wheatear
          from here to another;
stonechacker, snorter,
              from there to the other.

Brushing soil
from the baby's face,
resurfacing again;
like an owl drowned
in a cattle trough,
through the lutterings
and lettings of rain.

Wheatear, wheatear
          from one burrow to another;
horse masher, jobbler
              from here to the other.

And somewhere
in the chalk, in the folds
of her shawl;
three riders
on a bronze bull.

White arse, white arse
          from here to the other;
clodhopper, chichell
              from the dead to our mother.

Shaking the buried grain,
cradling the infant
like a hare
laid in a field
which comes
alive again.

iii

Cyclamen petals
on window sills
fade in exhaling light.
The hills have horses;

riderless
they graze freely
without the
paraphernalia of war.

And now
and again
they look up
from the bracken;

while women
bend attentive
sponging pale limbs,
talking in whispers.

iv

There is no weeping for a fox;
                    fur flat with rain,
shrunk over hunched ribs.

Propped against a fence post,
                    almost casual in its demise:
but without that warm black mollusc of a nose.

It is raining again from the north,
                    wind weaving flocks
of birds like withies:

an immigrant host, massed sodden heads,
                    pick through stubble
and red earth.

Where the barbel sit is bloody with soil:
                    and the river lays sediment
over new wheat.

November's bonfires rest unlit,
                    too late to encourage the sun:

the dead have been drawn back to the dead
                    and the bull is buried.

Omar Sabbagh

Breaths Between The Notes

Where it is to finish is not my business.
Where the gull flies, a parabola above a sea's miles
And miles, is taught me only by regrets,
How the scarecrows I know fall from my pockets
Like loose coins, like a flower's stray smells, a flower's ...

The island to the lone tree, the sky to the power
Of the happenstance made to dance to a styled
Essence, a thick thing-hood won by a swan's caress...

I can't offer more to the embossed choir –
A singe upon the chests of burly liars –
Than the architecture of my verse, muscular

Fire, and no wafting smoke to pillage and evict
What the air means, when by breeze it evokes
A sense of ending, and breaths between the notes.

Can I, Daddy: *Can I?*

For Mohamad Sabbagh

How round it is: to have a reach like the weather.
Here's a daring son, a sun-dance, petitions his father
For the second toy, the other, brightening the pure dark
Majesty of desire – like a brave, like a brazen metaphor ...

My deepest ploy at four years old: to be lavish and adored,
To gather that Moorish most that toys might ever afford
To give, in the slim and minute minute, the quick tour
Of childhood – urgent, rich, a silver of silver born...

And now, in the dirty, unwashed corner of the hour,
I'm like a man, still young, who roars at the flower
Of his youth – a wiseacre, bent-double, sour
With age, the wet wine of his life, reeking, off-the-mark –

A fallen acorn turned random, orphaned, laughed-at
By the mud. And a father, yes, the heart of a whitewater's
Raft, a galloping man, a grand piano and a grand craft
In the unspeaking corridors of a more song-soaked past.

Jonathan Taylor

Earworm

First those *flauti* triplets – then,

looping over and over again,
O terra, addio; addio valle di pianti,

a repetunitis *ad infinitum*,
sogno di gaudio che in dolor svanì...

and nothing can rid me of the *ohwurm*,
a noi si schiude il cielo e l'alme erranti,

neuronally condemned to G-flat major,
volano al raggio dell'eterno dì:

    and entombed in my synapses,
    voice in voice with Radamès,
    Aïda is still singing and dying,
    forever dying and loving,
    O terra, addio; addio valle di pianti,

while offstage, some chorus is intoning,
Immenso Fthà, noi t'invochiam,

now *piano*, now *pianissimio*,
now *pianississimo*,

and now gone.

Numeromania

And do you remember how for those miles and miles
of his Seventh Symphony I would walk you up and down,
every step a crotchet: *Allegro moderato, Adagio,
Sehr schnell, Bewegt doch nicht schnell*?

Perched on my shoulder, your three pounds shrieked louder
than an orchestra in E major. You were sometimes *piano*,
sometimes a wild *Scherzo*,

as I walked you up and down,
every step a crotchet: *Allegro moderato, Adagio,
Sehr schnell, Bewegt doch nicht schnell.*

And I thought of Bruckner and his counting mania,
flowers on women's dresses, leaves on trees,
notes, bars and phrases, windows in churches
to which he'd otherwise feel compelled to return,
footsteps he'd have to retrace,

walking up and down,
every step a crotchet: *Allegro moderato, Adagio,
Sehr schnell, Bewegt doch nicht schnell,*

no one crying on his shoulder.

Sally Festing

On reading *After A Journey*

What fancy charged you trace lost paths
through Autumn's dark –

to lead me to your first wife
with the new one on your arm?

Touching her face in every place
while making a voiceless ghost
your nutbrown eidolon

Jim Maguire

Neurasthenia

Russalka (destroyed), Henri Duparc, *1891*

(after Enzensberger)

He is back to himself again. Clicking his fingers
he takes Pushkin from the shelf. He ruminates.
He wastes time persuading Madame he is well enough
to be up and dressed. Just for today she lets him skip
the tepid sponging, the magneto-electric massage.
It is spring now. His music mind stirs with flitches of green
like the fiddleheads outside his window.
Clearing his throat, he will read aloud a verse,
feel the pull between the words and the music in his bones.
He will scrawl his motifs, impatiently, ghostlike,
on hand-drawn staves, set them off with skeletal harmonies.
He does too much and is forced to retire
to his room for weeks, dreams of a sweet embedding.
Then, at last – Easter has passed, and Pentecost –
he hauls the leatherbacked folio onto his desk
and starts to compose. This will be a redemptive score.
How do you compose a resurrection? The drowned girl
crystalising in the pampas as a river ghost, the fright
in the eyes of the boatmen, the hermit who's woken by the wind
reassembling echoes, love-talk ripping into his skin:
questions of key relations, problems of orchestration.
Dragging a lost muse from the mudflats is a difficult exercise.
Hardest to conjure are the smells – the sump where she rises,
the campfire smoke of his rags, her green cress lingerie...
To be real everything must be vaporised, everything
but the pages of his manuscript. His scheme is clear,
down to the appointed time: by St. Cecilia's Day
the river will be in spate, its perfumery scored
on a Wagnerian scale, gongs, a metallaphone
for dragging the drowned hermit's shadow
through underwater doors – incomplete chords

floating, nacreous corridors, a ballroom,
her boudoir ... while above on the shore, in mid-July,
promenaders will cling to their parasols and curse
the sudden downpour. The whole little rivertown en-fête
and only the composer remains inside. He looks alive.
Who would have thought that he, of all people,
could be so full of zest? Soaked, everything is soaked now,
aquamarine, uprushing energies converging in a kind
of manic clemency – except the score. It shrivels and darkens
as he finally sleeps, till the trademark floating motion is no more
than a dried-up rivulet. Dreaming of a first-night feast –
Fauré is there, and mother, miraculously come to life –
he stays oblivious; while Madame on tiptoe
pulls down his blinds, sends out for Nurse,
quietly tells the children to bring sticks for his fire.

Joey Connolly

Causality

(from a sequence)

Hypothesis: the post-rock soundtrack causes the scenery passing by the windows of the train.

An unexpected A minor seventh kicks up fountains
of Mountain Ash flamily from the passing hillside,
and the return to the persistent trudge of the F sharp
treads up a map of almost rusty heather from the Hope Valley's roll
like dust from a third-world track,
cracking in the heat like a sampled snare beating sevens
under the distorted fuzz of detuned guitars.

A bank of feedback shimmers to crescendo, so dense
a nylon-strung acoustic could strum safely into it,
be accommodated as background, its patterns
of almost atonal chords melting into static,
into a white noise which falls upon the Pennines:
a blanket early snow of Godspeed, or Mogwai,
or Silver Mount Zion,
                      or Explosions in the Sky.

Laurelyn Whitt

Tomboy

*Carriages are for dolls. Your
beautiful dolls. Only for dolls.
Remember.*

But I was not my mother's
daughter. Carriages
were for rocks. For
moving dirt

    or if conditions permitted,
    mud and water.

Despairing of my domestic potential
at six, mother tried again at
twelve
    with a sewing box.

*Scissors are for sewing, for
dresses and skirts. They are
not to be used otherwise.*

But otherwise was all there was:
her child wore pants, cut leather

made saddles for horse statues,
pouches for stones, cradleboards
out of old snowshoes.

It is all there still is:

grown now, the child sits,
sewing box on lap

removes the scissors   then
hesitates

before trimming silk flowers.

In that pause all that falls
between mothers and daughters
enters.

The scissors are heavy, in my hands.
I turn them, turn them.

Jane Clarke

Dressage

You find your seat by riding
without saddle or reins,
sit deep, fall off, get on again.

Give and take with lightness
of hand and leg, shift your weight
as you feel how she needs to move.

You find your rhythm by listening
to the sequence of hoofs,
count the beat of every stride.

Learn to read how she holds her head;
when to steady,
when to ask her to lengthen her pace

so the moment between lifting and falling
is held, sometimes so long
that together you don't touch the ground.

Robert Smith

Die Winterreise

His voice a lantern
lighting each blanketed milestone;
frost dislodged from a gatepost,
the lowliness of thorns;

and always the same outcome,
no matter its epic recital,
tramping through snows the piano
has already darkened.

Paul Wittgenstein

His one arm
grievous, prehensile,
rumbling up the keyboard,

arching itself for a treble
insuperably beyond reach,

the thumb on top
smudging the right hand's work –
his bunched musculature
digging out effort –

re-fingering Mendelssohn,
Schumann, Grieg – the repertoire
arduous in his head,

all heave and magnitude,
a tonnage of notes to be shifted
to new echelons,

ligaments matting
and mounded to the task,
the joints stringent, flourishes splayed open
spreadeagling octaves:

morose in repose,
shouldering his own embodiment,

he jemmies each key change,
the loose sleeve sulking with presentiments
of chords.

Sebastian Barker

A Treatise on Any Model of Being

'Questioning is the piety of thought.'
                                        Martin Heidegger

(Last two parts of A Poem in Twelve Movements)

Somewhere in Venezuela an ant took to looking through telescopes. His outlook
    on life was enlarged when he spotted an unknown galaxy. How many
    more? he wondered, as he sipped his G and T.
There, there, said the sheepdog, feed my sheep, feed my lambs. And the ant of the
    telescopes obeyed, because it was Good Friday.
Nowhere in the distance can we spot the tail of Being. It has vanished into the
    desert, somewhere south of Cairo, to contemplate the resurgence of
    scholastic interest in time.
For time like a baby sleeps in the cradle of God. Being is the nursemaid and
    mother rolled in one.
And time cries out with a hunger to start off the church bells of Europe. And
    nobody knows when they end, for time has become replete.
For time like a baby sleeps in the cradle of God.

                          *

Bring me to the house of Being, and I will give you language. There is no shorter
    route to the music of the spheres.
Twice I dropped my hymnbook. Twice I was forgiven. But what was I singing
    when the songs were open to all?
Can we measure bliss on a ruler? Does joy come in a packet? What is the price of
    Elysium? Or the Eleusinian mist?
Blow me a smoke-ring from your red lips, O Aphrodite. The nights in your arms
    are long, indeed they are ever-lasting.

So let me not forget to thank you for this enrapture, and our long curling dream
    together, which awakes in the bed of Being.
Fasten me to a rocket and I won't move at all.
I am a man asleep dreaming the dream of Being.
And everywhere there are reminders, like signposts in the sky.
Where shall I go with my message? Who will understand the ferocity out there?
Who will see the origin of energy in the chalice of the Aboriginal Being, who
    drinks from the chalice alone?
Cut me down to size and I'm no smaller. I do not walk on stilts. And clothes are a
    thing of the past. So is the past, of course. And the future. What of the
    Being that is? That is the one I choose.
Record my voice under the star-filled oak trees. I will be chanting tonight. And
    what I will be chanting is, 'A Treatise on Any Model of Being'.

Martin Bennett

Starlings

High then low above the pine-dark park
West of Stazione EUR-Palasport
X-thousand starlings flex their claim to be
The ultimate kinetic artists –

Against the blue, red, grey and violet
Of a late February sunset, picture
Split second Calder or Kandinsky,
Some sky-scrapering Jackson Pollock,

The whole of heaven his floor; next up
Is a calligrapher in silhouette –
Taking a holiday from blockish text,
He conjures an impromptu alphabet

Plus punctuation, pulsating fullstop,
Comma, colon, this exclamation mark
Which now out-tops the tallest treetop,
Now shrinks, its spiral turned speck.

Except, no sooner found than the metaphor's
Too slow, switched for an accordionist
Who unfolds crotchets, minims, quavers,
We groundling sight-readers of adjacent space.

Herinder Rai

The Candle

'I dream of painting and then I paint my dream'.

'I am still far from being what I want to be, but with God's help I shall succeed. I want to be bound to Christ with unbreakable bonds and to feel these bonds. To be sorrowful yet always rejoicing'. Vincent Van Gogh

Tormented in day, a yearning tallow –
until heavenly light burns barren sky;
'Night, ignite! Ignite, your tarnished halo –
deliverance is yours!' the seraphs cry.
(O bittersweet release! The shackled are free!)
The brightest fires console the darkest chills,
and I exist – though raging flames consume me –
brush flickering intently with free will.
Love's tinder lingers in hopeful air …
a divine call for all times and weather –
mandatory trust; unquenchable flare
extinguishable yes, but not forever!

All is forgiven when tomorrow redeems
the painted stars and scars of sorrowed dreams.

Jay Ramsay

Requiescat in Pace

for my father, July 2007

The room still. Just the ceiling fan whirring
You lie on your back now in profile
turned from the curled right side of your dying
your left hand placed over your stomach
a sprig of rosemary on your chest.

Your mouth still open with its last breath
as if to breathe in again and speak
eyes closed instead in the bruise of their declivity
your face at peace, and more than peace
gathered as if to a point between your eyes
as you leap beyond all you've ever been
into all you ever really are –
like a salmon leaping at the falls.

Now you show me how we are
absolutely not our personality
but strange as we've seldom been seen
now I'm seeing there are two sides to your face
separated as if by an invisible line
marked by the rosemary: Left side, nearest
you still recognizably saying 'Ah –'
so I can almost hear you
endless where the breath travels
over and over breathed out again and silent.
And on the other side, window side
you have become a perfect stranger
other, Oriental, warrior out of time
as if from another life become this life
at all its height and secret depth
risen like an extraordinary mosaic
into all the contours of your face
proclaiming *I am the Self that is here*.

I gaze and gaze between standing and sitting
crossing from one side of the bed to the other
your whole body the imprint of what is left
in this final movement of your spirit; and father
I am your witness at last. Your mystery
fills my eyes with more than tears, as mine will fill me.
And as I try to find a way to say goodbye
all I feel is greeting.

Tim Murdoch

Amicitia

Whatever we touched
survives today
through all estranging
circumstance, the play
of particles,
the weather, the delay.

The thing once learned
is long forgotten now,
its ordering event –
electron muon tau –
still capers through us
both (they don't say how) –

hurls us into space,
no more friend and friend
swearing a vow,
but keen to comprehend
a moment come to pass
that didn't end.

Whoever we were:
the difference unseen
by converging souls;
the pattern in the screen
around us, defines
a bond of King and Queen.

Masks

I talk all day about listening
and still don't listen enough.

Tonight you're quieter than ever;
the call of the wood-pigeon
emphasising a sultry pause among
the trees you're tented by

pondering, expecting I shall
mistake you again for a friend
I knew but never understood,

an acrobatic swift cartwheeling
into a cloud, or the dragonfly
that sped quickly from my hand,
making me wonder if delight
was merely perpetual surprise.

Susan Wicks

United Enemies

Thomas Schütte, 4-colour offset print 69 x 98.6 cm

Is he like Janus, does he look this way
and also to the future?
And what can his blind twin
be dreaming, face to the black sky?

They are two continents drifting apart
as far as their flesh will let them:
two heads that once used to fit
jawbone to aching jawbone, skull to skull –

the averted forehead of Brazil
to the Gulf of Guinea, Nova Scotia's cheek
to the brow of Morocco. Slowly they veer
into dark. And will never come back

or fully leave, tied as they both are
to a single shrinking body under glass,
the way that brute in Virgil – was it Mezentius? –
would torture captives, every living face

crushed close to a dead one. And this creature knows
how the gods shuffle their creased birds
and lightning bolts and flames and let them flutter
down into blue – how knowledge dies.

Curtains

for Holly Downing

This is an old light,
where the gleam along a pleat
is geometric, and the shadowed rest
waits somewhere beyond the canvas:
how the painter loved
these fabrics, more than what they dressed

in shining folds; how they glow and steal
life from the flat flesh
and have survived. These surfaces
the painter used to touch,
this linen, silk and velvet,
are her true subject.

They are more themselves than skin;
sloughed, the crumpled cloth
mimics a white smile, a laugh,
lies crumpled on a shelf
or droops from the wooden cliff
to make a painted lap with peaks and troughs.

They are their own stuff
falling, only the draped window
ours, the scenes from ordinary life,
the play, the picture. Even the bed
we all stand round. And these are red
and gold and emerald, and closed on love.

Daniel K. Lee

In the Dark

Not just mine, but your intentions stain in the dark.
Re-christened 'temptation', gathers like rain in the dark.

By what regime of lotion, genes, or god, are
such soft slopes justified in being vain in the dark?

Smash the dinner plates for this extinguished distance!
I'll pour the shots, darling, to drain in the dark.

The clothes measure a man? Says who: when patterns
from paisleys to pinstripes are all plain in the dark.

O blameless boy, of the bare way we failed you:
you were, with no wind, a weathervane in the dark.

Wherever God's hiding the cure for your death sentence,
for you I'm overturning every grain in the dark.

When all else is hijacked, I'll leave you the hymn.
The ear never loses the refrain in the dark.

Is the dark pitiless to prolong the punishment?
Reliving your whisper is worth the pain in the dark.

Before caving in to lips pursed into an apology,
give me a chance to at least complain in the dark.

Silence – be warned – is a consummate politician:
an ally in light, bane in the dark.

A toast to ignorance for prolonging bliss!
Why sober a thrill if we remain in the dark?

I fall into fantasy. How do I know? You are saying,
'This word *yours*, Daniel, could you explain ...in the dark?'

Jay Rogoff

All the Same

Spinning *Cosi*, Penny ponders. 'Mozart
slays me. I'd fall for a guy aged 250
who understood a girl like Fiordiligi.
What the heart hurts to learn! If I lose heart
God let me lose it to a man whose art
seduces me with such sincerity
that even when it lies – say, poetry
concocted by some Don Giovanni upstart –
I might pretend his groaning sonnet's genuine
as if scrawled from a vein, no sham designs
to make me lie with feelings – and me – full peeled.'
Joy conceives when art plots to bare our ends.
'All the same, meeting you on that softball field,
boy, I could swear that you were born Albanian.'

Travesty

Franco-Prussian War, 1870

Rosa Bonheur's trousers served
her bravely: horse fairs, abbatoirs,
tromping stench, mud, merde, blood to sketch
horses, cows – yet no outfit called

her to fight. Bobbed hair, Gauloises,
she tricked the townsfolk: 'See the sweet
little old man? Once sang in Rome,
St. Peter's last castrato.'

Eugénie Fiocre swaggered. She'd
spent half her Opéra career in pants.
Androgynous colonel thrusting with her blade,
she led her buxom squadron to romance
the shapely spouses of a remote village
whose husbands ran off on a drinking tour,
leaving their hungry wives swooning onstage,
fancying Eugénie's posterior
a saddle fit for riding into war.

The war made Rosa Bonheur itch to fight.
She drilled with rifles, marched with macho neighbours –
rejected! unlike Marie-Antoinette
Lix, who rose to lieutenant of sharpshooters.

In France war crossed lines into travesty.
Bonheur petitioned the police for legal
permission to wear pants, not for her passion
for panting breasts,
unspeakable in 1870,
but braving slaughterhouse and stableyard,
treading blood and filth as on the field
of battle – for painting beasts.
In a single bird, *The Wounded Eagle*,
she fantasized the plummet of the Prussian
army, amazed at Rosa mailed, saint-slender
and blazing in sun-dazzle, legendary
Joan reborn and spurring France to glory.

The Hunt

Sorana Santos, chosen young essayist

Inextricable Links

In western culture, old English folk tales, or Cante-Fables as they are known, are, as their name suggests, stories half spoken and half sung. At a point in history the Cante-Fables split to become what we know now as folk songs and folk tales – a parallel to what some theorise to be how language and music developed. Similarly, the Portuguese call their national song, Fado,'Poemas Cantadas', or, sung poems. There are also remarkable examples of cultures for whom words and music are both one and the same, such as the U'wa culture of Colombia that to this day communicate and transfer the knowledge and history of their culture solely through song. In Mandarin, a tonal language, meaning is dependent on the perception of pitch, it is even possible to entertain audiences by playing music that has a 'spoken meaning'.[1] There are more examples of how deeply embedded the link between music and language is in human communication, and more still are the number of academic disciplines researching the causality of this phenomenon.

Historical Musicologists have long established that:

> The human voice and hands are the principal means for linguistic expression but also the earliest musical instruments... A vocal apparatus sufficient for the production of sustained singing has been estimated as arriving perhaps 1.5 million years ago. Percussive hands have been around longer.[2]

The evolution of language is undoubtedly highly intertwined with the evolution of music [3] despite there being much debate as to whether they evolved alongside or separately from one another. On one hand, one body of evidence suggests that the further we go back prehistorically, the more speech resembles song until primeval man's first tone and expression had

---

[1] Ehrenfeld, Temma, *Between Speech and Song Observer* Vol.24, No.10, December 2011
[2] Frayer & Nicolay, *Fossil Evidence for the Origin of Speech Sounds,* in Wallin, Merker & Brown, *The Origins of Music,* 2000
[3] Brown, Merker, & Wallin, *An Introduction to Evolutionary Musicology,* MIT Press, Cambridge, 2000

no differentiation whatsoever between song and speech, which supports the notion of language evolving from music.[4] On the other, the opposing stance, led by the well-known linguist, Steven Pinker, asserts that music developed as an appendage to language itself, alluded to beautifully in his famous quote:

> As far as biological cause and effect are concerned, music is useless. It shows no signs of design for attaining ... accurate perception ... of the world. Compared with language ... music could vanish from our species and the rest of our lifestyle would be virtually unchanged. Music appears to be ... a cocktail of recreational drugs that we ingest through the ear to stimulate a mass of pleasure circuits at once.[5]

While perhaps cold and limited, this statement can be seen to reflect our society's attitude to the arts and consequently art's function within society, since we find their numerous beneficial aspects (discussed below) either sidelined or outweighed in favour of commerce.

Pinker's statement aside, human beings have been drawn to sounds near the boundary of speech and song throughout history, from 'devotional chants, and speeches, [to] ... rap music'. Diana Deutsch, whose research specialises in the cognitive perception of music and language also states that:'Poets and lyricists are our practical experts on the boundary ... because they arrange words to enhance our perception of musical qualities.'[6]

Musicians themselves have similarly perceived this relationship. Janacek dedicated four decades of his life to spoken and melodic transcriptions in addition to the folk music collections he is famed for, and, according to biographer Zemanova: 'Janáček wished to investigate the music of language rather than the language of music.'[7]. Mendelssohn also closely considered this relationship, famously saying that:

> People often complain that music is too ambiguous, that what they should think when they hear it is so unclear, whereas everyone understands words. With me it is exactly the opposite, and not only with regard to an entire speech but also with individual words. These too seem to me so ambiguous, so vague, so easily misunderstood in

---

[4] Steiner, Rudolf, *Speech and Song,* Lecture transcription, Dornach, December 2nd 1922
[5] Pinker, Steven, *How the Mind Works,* Norton Press, New York, 1999
[6] Deutsch, Diana, op.cit
[7] Janáček, Leos. As cited in Zemanova, Mirka, ed. & trans, *Janáček's Uncollected Essays on Music,* 1989

comparison to genuine music, which fills the soul with a thousand things better than words.[8]

We see that music and language both also play a significant role in regards to child development. Mothers the world over sing to their children as early as they speak to them, and it has been proven that both song and instrumental music are vital tools in developing linguistic ability in young children. The El Sistema programme which runs in South America and the UK provides strong evidence year-on-year that music boosts not only the literacy and social skills of young children, but also makes an overwhelmingly positive contribution to the development of independence, school attendance and overall achievement,[9] with student groups achieving higher reading and comprehension scores after musical training.[10] It has also been shown that 'the longer the duration of the music training ... the better the verbal memory'[11] and that 'adults with music training in their childhood demonstrate better verbal memory.'[12]

In neuroscience, research has also identified connections between auditory-processing skills and verbal-processing skills. Nina Kraus' research into this relationship showed that musicians have better connections between their auditory and verbal processing, and also that brain waves resemble the sound wave which it is perceiving,[13] and so it is reasonable to assume that the same may be true for language.

In his famous string quartet 'Different Trains', which samples fragments of experiences given by evacuees of the Second World War, Steve Reich imitates the exact intonation of the sampled speech in individual string parts. One particular study by Diana Deutsch which looked at whether we hear repeated segments of speech as speech or sound, found that when isolating and repeating a phrase, it 'suddenly appears to burst into song ...'[14]. John Cage said: 'What makes something music or language is the way our minds interpret it ...' and, albeit unintentionally, Reich's use of this auditory illusion

---

[8] Machlis, Forney, *The Enjoyment of Music*, Tenth Edition, Norton Press, New York, 1999

[9] http://www.ihse.org.uk/results

[10] *The Impact of Music on Language & Early Literacy*, http://www.abcmusicandme.com/documents/Impact_of_Music_on_Literacy.pdf, p.1

[11] Ho, Cheung & Chan, *Music Instruction aids Verbal Memory*, The American Psychological Association, 2003

[12] Chan et al, *Links between Musical Learning and Reading*, Journal of Humanities and Social Science, 1998

[13] Kraus, N., & Chandrasekaran, B. *Music Training for the Development of Auditory Skills*, Nature Reviews *Neuroscience*, 11, p.599

[14] Deutsch, Diana, *The Speech to Song Illusion*, University of California, 1995

is a strong artistic representation of Deutch's research since it makes use of the necessary isolation and repetition a phrase requires to transform it from speech to song.

The aspects of music that allow us to identify whether music is sad have also been found to be present in speech.[15] Songs we consider to be sad will often start with a distance between two notes known by musicians as a minor third – think 'Greensleeves' – and it is widely accepted that there is enough evidence to suggest that language and music 'share resources' at certain neural processing levels.[16]

Artistically too, both music and language can express themselves in almost identical ways, sharing both terminology – pitch, rhythm, timbre, tempo, phrasing, intonation, timing, delivery/performance – and transcription techniques. Yet despite this we have come to a point where these two media that share so much in common, appear much more distinct to one another than they are due to their written form.

Looking at the subject from my own personal experience as a composer and writer, I can see that going back to my primary school scrawlings, nothing seemed to make more sense than to work with both music and language, sometimes together, and sometimes not. I also remember being told that I had to specialise, and that no one who did more than one thing ever did it well, and yet I couldn't help but compose *and* write. I also happen to be a sound-colour synesthete which means I hear sound as colour, and often catch myself looking for the right colour words for a phrase in a poem or the 'right colour' mode, sound, or chord for a piece; my synesthesia does not discriminate between speech and music.

Whether working with language and/or music to construct my work, I like to give close attention to constructing a clear the 'line' or 'thread' that carries the work through from beginning to end, regardless of whether it is atonal, arrhythmic or asymmetric musically or linguistically – these forms can still carry 'lines' of sorts within them. I am a stickler for technique and am fascinated by the structural approaches in twentieth century composition and literature, as well as those found in twelfth century Japan and Malaysia, and I enjoy cross-applying structural norms across poetry, prose, composition, and song. At times this produces rather unworkable, nonsensical results, but there are many occasions in which the results tease a boundary just enough to satisfy my curiosity.

---

[15] Curtis, Megan, *Music and Speech Share A Code* http://blogs.scientificamerican.com/observations/2010/06/17/music-and-speech-share-a-code-for-c-2010-06-17/

[16] Patel, Aniruddh et al, *Processing Syntactic Relations in Language and Music*, Journal of Cognitive Neuroscience, 1998

Songwriting always felt like the opportunity to explore the balance of one medium against another, not just sonically, but visually also. Perhaps owing to my study of composition I never felt constrained by the use of conventional structures. I like to give attention to the extent to which lyrics might stand as a poetic work in their own right, and enjoy toying with how presenting a song score with a strong aleatoric (chance) element can alter the listener's perspective on a work that could have been perceived as through-composed.

What I am appreciating most about the New Music Industry is the freedom it presents those with less conservative and commercial approaches to songwriting to flourish outside of the mainstream and genre-defined cultures and connect directly to their audience, exploring concepts in songwriting that go beyond what we currently believe is possible and/or viable. There is much to be explored in this area and I find myself wondering the extent to which commercialisation has stunted the development of this art form and what new genre might exist as an after-work bedroom project; what cannot be exploited for monetary gain is seen as having no worth, and so often remains unseen. However, the wider impact of music's emerging business models is yet to be fully realised, and the potential for the research into the artistic relationship between words and music to be brought into society through these models has arrived.

CHOSEN BROADSHEET POETS

Benjamin Jack Larner (b.1990) is a London-based composer and poet. He was awarded an entrance scholarship to study Composition at the Royal Academy of Music, London, and was the recipient of the Arthur Hervey Scholarship upon his graduation in the summer of 2013. Recent musical works include *Three Declarations of Love*, a setting of texts from Shakespeare's *King Lear* for Mezzo-Soprano and Symphony Orchestra, and *Two Blake Songs* for Mezzo-Soprano and Double Bass. His poetry has previously featured in issues 18 and 19 of the *Agenda Online Broadsheet*, and he was one of the featured *Broadsheet poets* invited to read at the 2012 *Agenda International Poetry Festival* in Sussex. He is the grandson of acclaimed Irish poet, Desmond O'Grady, who has a long association with *Agenda*.

Circe

The Sea gifts years or honey.
Honey, gifts, or years to
Ivory of recitation provide
Chrysalid Resonance.

Illuminated Script.

Repetition moulded passage
Passage moulded repetition,
Towards and towards

… and tomorrow.

… and the heather bent in
slowed ecstasy a face again
a face again
a face again

and the heather …

Manifold recitations provide
Observations again sculpture.

Resonant growth.

Sedentary growth.

Tall and strong and

Swaddling.

AGAIN! AGAIN!

And the Sea gifts years or honey.
Honey, gifts, or years.

Years or honey or
Salt or seeds or

AGAIN! AGAIN!

Sediment or…

AGAIN!

… and the heather is bent in
*slowed ecstasy a face again
a face again
a face again…*

Resonant is ivory to
Sculpture and script
Moulded and repetition
And honey and
Repetition and
Repetition and
Towards and
Towards and
Tomorrow.

*We shall wait full lungs
And long grass
And purple fingers*

*…the heather is bent in
slowed ecstasy a face again
a face again
a face again*

and the heather...

Illuminated plaster built with honey,
Thickening blood,
Again sculpture again
Script moulded repetition.

AGAIN! AGAIN!

Gifts the Sea,

The Sea.

A passage of plastered ivory
Gifts the Sea.

The Sea.

AGAIN! AGAIN!

Passage moulded Sea
Towards and towards
And towards...

...and we shall wait full lungs

and long grass

and purple fingers

a face again
a face again
and we shall wait

a face again

and long grass

and purple fingers

and we shall wait

and we shall wait

and we shall wait

The Shadow Man

(two extracts)

i

My Darling Silver Moon,

                The supple brush to darkened gait,
    I think that we should hold hands this evening.
       Be not aware of the watching waters,
             Or the willow's guide;
         We are, as to each other, a star.

                           A stone.

                        An apple.

            I have only read in blue,
          My golden spring.

     Unearth this body, and I shall drown.

Yours,

      Always yours,

           Always…

ii

                           The shawl is spread.

                    Touching the pond
            Rippled eyes, chaste of sleep.

        Bronze coloured.

              Weathered green betwixt water and
        Wind grazed soil, afresh with
                May shoots and buds.

       O perform no acts
          Bitter, sweet or beautiful, child.

Child, for whom the cyclic heavens rotate.

              Your voice leaks an opulence,
             Radiant in the morning dew.

    Each voice, a carried form.
      Each voice, design emblazoned birth.

Solitude's paramour.
    Lone prism of rose-water light.

Mvt III - Cordelia

From the score of *Three Declarations of Love* (settings from *King Lear*), music by Ben Larner

Sorana Santos, 30, is an award-nominated composer and writer who gained her first degree in Composition under the tutelage of Diana Burrell at the Guildhall School of Music and Drama. She has been published worldwide as both a musician and writer and her first book, *Posthumous: Poems through the Concepts of Contemporary Music*, is due for publication by Lazy Gramophone Press.

Bone Ritual

Forgive me father for I do but sin.
Deny all flesh and pleasure to my lips
And take my precious bones in sallow skin,
To Adam to reclaim that granted rib.

Deny all flesh and pleasure to my lips
As so entwined were we in lip and gut
That at this altar with its black ellipse
I cough His bones out when I double up.

So entwined were we in lip and gut
That I could blow my wishes through his veins
And cough his bones out when I doubled up
To resurrect the covenant again.

That I could blow my wishes out these veins!
But too impure am I, so genuflect
To resurrect that covenant again
and neither raise the cup nor break the bread.

But too impure am I to genuflect
So take this creed to scour my purity
and neither raise the cup nor break the bread
To further resurrect the life in me.

I take this creed to scour my purity,
In penance pray for puritan marrow
To further resurrect the life in me,
So dance for Him until my ribs are showing

In penance, pray for puritan marrow
And purge confessional on bended knee,
Then dance for him until my skin is sallow
In hope, like Eve, to fend shame with a leaf.

Purge my confessional on bended knee
When the rite of Courtly Love wears thin.
Soon, like Eve, I'll fend shame with a leaf,
This body: it is given up for Him.

At last the rite of Courtly Love's worn thin,
And hidden is my faith beneath these robes;
This body, which is given up for him
Has made a ritual of casting stones.

Hidden is my faith beneath these robes…
Forgive me father for I do but sin.
Make a ritual of casting stones,
And take my precious bones in sallow skin.

Ocean

When from that depth where I revealed this life, my crest,
And from that vantage point there I discerned that hymn,

An echo tumbled slowly and I was undressed,
Disrobed, my nakedness fixed its concern with Him.

And follow… how I followed! Like the rocket's tail!
Sparkling, effervescent, down, as sterns did sing,

That sailor who could catch the wind without a sail,
In tides that drew us under and spurned us within.

The storms that broke the surface when our currents crossed,
The nights I drew back deepest – when I learned to swim –

Forged a stronger wave from out those lowest troughs,
That left no stone unturned that was not turned for Him.

Yet shallow! How so shallow are His ripples cast?
The depths at which He coasts have been adjourned by Him.

That is not His mascot that sits atop His mast,
Now I, a vessel, have been overturned by Him.

To sink with shadows to the depths, or reappear?
No blaze of glory roared that did not burn for Him.

But I am – and so exist – as salt and tears,
In ebbing and in flow I only yearn for Him.

So wallow… how I wallowed in those haunted pools,
Whilst seagulls swooped and swerved and sang nocturnes for Him,

And I lapped softly at the rocks for molecules,
Of that wave broken too soon, once more to turn to Him.

Not consecrated with the wearing of a ring,
But celebrated with the sacred urn and hymn,

When seers stargaze to the depths of the ocean,
And mariners cast good eyes on Saturnine rings,

And even swallows fly that they may mate and thaw,
And man makes miracles that show us worm with limb,

Yet never was there wave that could remain ashore,
And broken now, once more, I will return to Him.

Kim Moore's first pamphlet *If We Could Speak Like Wolves* was a winner in the 2012 Poetry Business Pamphlet Competition and was named as a Book of the Year in the *Independent*. She won an Eric Gregory in 2011 and a Geoffrey Dearmer Prize in 2010. She works for Cumbria Music Service as a Brass Teacher.

The Musicians

drag themselves to afternoon rehearsal.
They're paid to be there but still resent it.
The brass section are getting restless –
the conductor has gone ten minutes over time.

They would rather be eating at the pub
or having a drink before the concert starts.
The average trumpet player is just past
middle age, balding and divorced

used to being alone, this is the most social
thing he does, but still he would rather end it.
The trombones start to be obnoxious,
play loudly to piss the violas off.

At the pub talk turns to kit, mouthpieces,
reverse lead pipes, and the brass, as usual,
cut it fine before they're back, getting changed
in the vestry, while the violins are tuning up

and suddenly with the orchestra in black,
everyone looks different and when the choir
start to sing and the violins begin,
and the trumpets and trombones and horns

lay down their blocks of sound
for the voices to hang onto,
I admit, if I was in the audience,
I'd think we were enjoying it.

Being a Trumpet Teacher

I say: imagine you are drinking a glass of air.
Let the coldness hit the back of your throat.

Raise your shoulders to your ears, now let
them be. Get your cheeks to grip your teeth.

Imagine you are spitting tea leaves
from your tongue to start each note

so each one becomes the beginning of a word
Sing the note inside your head then match it.

At home lie on the floor and pile books
on your stomach to check your breathing.

Or try and pin paper to the wall just by blowing.
I say: remember the man who played so loud

he burst a blood vessel in his eye. This was
because he was drunk (although I don't tell

them that). I say it was because he was young,
and full of himself, and far away from home.

Ode to my Trumpet on the First Year of its Retirement

I did not set out to make a year of it,
it was unannounced, it was unarranged
but it's been twelve months since
I played more than C, D, E, F and G on you,

it's been a year since I played
anything but elderly quavers
chugging along to a backing track
in the concert key of Bb major

or more often, crotchets
at less than walking pace
or semibreves to demonstrate
how a note should be straight

'like' I say 'when you are practising
your handwriting, and each letter
must sit on the line, as if your words
were people on a bus seat,

this is how your note should rest
in the air without dipping
or over-reaching itself' and this
is the most I've let you do all year.

I have not taken you to church
and sat in the cold with you tucked
in my coat so your tuning is steady.
I have not brought you to the pub

and left you in the corner
like a walking stick or umbrella.
I have not taken you to the pit
of a theatre with the creak

of the stage floor above both
our heads, with the dark
and the stand lights flickering.
We have not played an encore this year.

I have not practised my double
or my triple tonguing, my intervals,
my slurring. You have lived in the car
all year, the world's most obedient dog,

you still go everywhere with me,
my palm still remembers the shape
of your casing, my arms still remember
your length and your weight I know

by heart – but I have not spoken to you
at all, I have not taken you to pieces
and cleaned each separate part.
Forgive me. I've not thought of you till now.

NOTES FOR BROADSHEET POETS

Martin Kratz
Words and music, land and sea: On writing a first libretto

The Mermaid of Zennor is a story rooted in a place where the borders between land and sea are constantly shifting and shaping each other. When he lived there from 1914-1916, D. H. Lawrence wrote a score of letters trying to convince his friends, Katherine Mansfield and John Middleton Murray, to move to Cornwall with him. 'It is a most beautiful place,' he writes, 'a tiny granite village nestling under high, shaggy moorhills, and a big sweep of lovely sea beyond, such a lovely sea, lovelier even than the Mediterranean. ... It is all gorse now, flickering with flower; and then it will be heather; and then hundreds of foxgloves.'[1]

Going there today, it feels as if little has changed. I visited in early May to research the libretto for a chamber opera based on the legend and had a small dorm in the Youth hostel all to myself. I saw few other tourists the whole time I was there. The large bay windows of my room looked out onto exactly the scene Lawrence described. The fields extended towards the sea, then opened onto it completely where the gorse fell away. The actual meeting point between land and sea was out of sight, tucked under the cliffs. I knew, that hidden there, lay Pendour Cove, the place where the mermaid, Morveren, had been resting when she first heard the evening hymn being sung by the fisherman Matthew Trewhella in the local church:

> God be praised for if we drown we know
> your loving warmth waits in the depths below.
> The rising sun will see us back aboard
> casting our nets out in your name O Lord.
> (from *The Mermaid of Zennor – A Chamber Opera*)

The hymn is the starting point for the legend. In a reversal of the classic siren myth, Matthew's beautiful singing draws Morveren onto land. Every day she visits the church in disguise, lingering in the pews a little longer each time, but always leaving before the end of the service. Inevitably, one evening

---

[1] Kinkead-Weekes, Mark. 1996. *D.H. Lawrence: triumph to exile, 1912-1922, Volume 1*. (Cambridge: Cambridge University Press)

she stays too long and stumbles as she tries to rush away. She accidentally exposes her tail to the hostile congregation, but Matthew in turn has fallen in love with the beautiful stranger and accompanies her back under the sea. A traditional ending has it, that their singing can sometimes still be heard over the waves.

It is easy to believe in the story of the mermaid when you are in Zennor. There is so much traffic between land and sea, gifts being shuttled back and forth: mist, dust, the toll of the church bell. Why not messages, or a song? The wind kept me up all night, clattering against the shutters, so perhaps I was mostly sleep-drunk, but while I was in Zennor, the ethereal elements of the story gradually assumed the shape of hard facts. The hymn for instance, suggested its own form, rhythm and content. In the traditional story, Matthew is specified as being a tenor. If you listened for it, you could hear the story offering its own operatic potential.

> We have lingered in the chambers of the sea
> By sea-girls wreathed with seaweed red and brown
> Till human voices wake us, and we drown.
> (from 'The Love Song of J. Alfred Prufrock')

So writes T.S. Eliot, and it does feel, when you are writing about mermaids, that some sort of anchor in reality is needed. Standing on the South West Coast Path, looking down on Pendour Cove, the sharp snap of the edges of my cagoule in the wind must have crept into this thinking. The cag-clad, hiking-booted Walker would become one of the key characters in the libretto. In our modern retelling, it is she who finds Matthew washed up on the shore, concussed and confused, and acts as the one-foot-in-reality, the voice of scepticism as he recollects the series of events, which lead him there. 'I know this bay. These cliffs. This strand,' he says, 'I know this cove, the black stone stained / by the ocean-fret.' He knows it, because it has not changed in the hundreds of years he has been underwater. I could not quite reach the bay itself from the path, but I knew that if someone were to wash up there, it would be impossible to shout up for help. You would be instantly drowned out by the wind, the tossing of the sea. The cliffs, sloped and curled like an amphitheatre, would almost certainly block a mobile phone signal. Eventually, the cliffs would be played by the audience, and the tumble of rocks on the sand by the small orchestra, heavy on wind section and percussion. The mermaid was there too that day, hidden by the rocks, present in her absence.

This, I learned, happens to the words in a libretto too: they become present in their absence. In a Q&A after a talk I gave with the composer Leo Geyer on creating the opera, I was asked quite bluntly, why, as a librettist, I was there that evening. No one remembered an opera for the words. The only thing that mattered was the music. It is a question every librettist must be prepared to answer. A libretto is not like a poem, which has learned to stand on its own, and draw its entire strength from its own rhythm and form. An opera with terrible music will not survive no matter how good the writing is. So, a libretto can feel like a half-thing, which will not be anything until it is set to music. Mozart referred to the poetry in opera as music's obedient daughter. Perhaps, the sense that the poetry serves the music is not an entirely bad one, but it does not really allow for any subtlety, any exchange in the relationship. To my mind, Benjamin Britten comes much closer when he says to his librettist Myfanwy Piper of the words in a libretto: 'Don't colour them. The music will do that.'[2] In this sense, the words support the music, but do not encroach on it where they are not needed.

What I put to my questioner, is that without the libretto, there would be no opera in the first place. If the libretto has done its job properly, then the words inspire the music; and this is only their first job. The libretto continues to support the music even after it has been composed. The librettist and poet Michael Symmons Roberts gave me the advice, that no matter what the composer does musically, a strong libretto undergirds the whole piece with an underlying integrity. It can achieve this for instance through regularity in form. If the integrity is not there, even with strong music, the opera at that point will feel weak. The words also support the singers. In rehearsal, I came across the tenor repeating Matthew's line 'shell splinters bite into my skin'. He told me it was his favourite line, because in this very charged scene, in which Matthew is desperately trying to remember who he is, the consonants give the singer something to hold onto.

The Mermaid of Zennor returns again and again to the point where land and sea meet, probing the borderland, asking where one begins and the other ends. The tension between land and sea is equally the tension between words and music, and this libretto if it is about anything, is about writing a first libretto. Perhaps every first libretto is about writing a first libretto, and must necessarily ask how words and music can be related to each other in a meaningful way. For me, the dynamic is best illustrated back in Pendour Cove, there at the point at which the line is first drawn between sea and land. In fact, it happens, if we let ourselves zoom in, just on the sea's side rather than the land's side, just there, where before it is obscured by deep blue and green, you can still recognise the sand through the water, carrying it, but all you hear is ocean.

---

[2] Piper, Myfanwy. 1979. 'Writing for Britten', in *The Operas of Benjamin Britten*, ed. by Peter Pears (London: Hamish Hamilton) pp. 8-21

Sebastian Barker

Judging Poetry

For Merrily Harpur

'Another middle-age departure
Of Apollo from the trade of archer.'
                Patrick Kavanagh, 'Prelude'

i

A poem is a thing I am looking for.
It has its own shape, its own content, its own warmth, its own music, and its own way of being in the world.
A poem is an animate entity.
It is a creature seen in a forest: a creature that, on inspection, is most definitely alive.
It is a creature who talks to me.
Who converses on every level I place before it.
A poem is a thing, a courtroom of soul, where matter coheres with meaning, and the judgement of the day is satisfaction.
Because a poem is a thing, a living creature who talks to us, when I pass judgement, as in a judge in a poetry competition,
I am looking for this beast in the forest, this animalman at home in its own ecology.
The poem has come full grown from its unique evolution through the annals of language.
It is a grown-up voice that knows how to pronounce itself.
The poem reaches out and behaves with perfect manners in a room full of other poems.

ii

Poetry chisels the word to an empty mansion into which something like the sun rises, speaking its luminous parables.
A poem is a ewe with her lamb chewing the grass touched by the light of heaven in a poet's mind.
A poem is the marriage ring between the lovers of life.
Poetry does not aim at political correctness; it arrives on the bandwagons

transporting successful partygoers wooed by the many politicians.
A poem can travel through six inches of steel like a hand through mist.
The creation of steel itself is unquestionably poetic.
Steel pours from stone, like rivers of fire down a volcano.
Poetry is an objective fact, like a bolt from the blue when falling in love.
It requisitions logic, like a king soldiers.

iii

Waterfalls recall it, a vaporising image of something thunderous.
You can slap it on a table, presenting a book full of it – a book no one can open without scales falling from our eyes.
There is a tempo to poetry, which is the tempo of the heart beating.
No one dissects it, not even a critic, poring over the black holes in his own invention.
There is a subject-matter to poetry which is not explicit: the poet like the reader sees a vision, an insubstantial vision, which is nevertheless necessarily there.
This is true of the poem 'Jerusalem', which brings down to earth the possibility of –
'And did those feet in ancient time'.

iv

Were it not for poetry, governments would direct the soul.
Plato knew this, which is why he feared it.
When governments recite poetry, beware, for the inauthentic is the short-cut to hell.
Across the fiery waters into the Greek inferno, the poets stroll, some arm-in-arm, with even the great mystery of life and death perhaps a subject for jokes.
For poets are the pragmatics of thinking.
What they think is what they create.
And what they create is what God creates through them.
For poets are God's fountain pens, his incandescent computers printing out the complexities of subatomic particles and moral decency.

v

Poetry does not butter up its admirers.
The admirers of poetry are those who are full of sense.
And what we sense in our poets is the fragrance of a perfume only to be
 sniffed on the other side of the path perilous
On any ascent up the magic mountain.
For inauthentic poetry is immoral, the gorgeous virgin turned malodorous
 slut, cut wings pasted to a dead phalanx of words.
And what of the poems fallen in unattended orchards, the rotting apples that
 might have fed thousands?
What do we know of unborn and unknown poems?
There is, in theory, no limit to their number.

vi

Plato loved poetry, poets, and poems tuned to the heavenly – but most
 definitely not tuned to the ungodly and the wicked.
Poetry is therefore a medium through which both good and evil may flow,
 like history through an accurate memory.
The main point about poetry is that it is the tie-up between man and God,
 God and man.
When poetry fails, reach for your torch, for we will all be travelling in
 darkness.
When it succeeds, there is nothing like it, because we have the end of a
 string
Which instructs us through the dark labyrinth into immaculate spaces.

vii

Poetry is the campus of the king and queen of heaven.
It is the university where the university is taught.
Bells roll over fields: it is the summer: birds are the lyrical masterpiece of
 June.
As joy sinks into a haystack, so does poetry twinkle in the streams.
Poetry shines in the light of nature, like a bride by her wedding altar.
Poetry comes to a soul like a flower into blossom, like a tree into blossom,
Like the unfolded rose into the buttonhole of a bridegroom.

viii

Poetry is not rhyme and reason, logic and learning, mathematics and
       marshmallows: it is all of these
Dancing in a starry night to a band of inspired musicians.
It rocks and it rolls.
It has the temperature and feel of adult love.
There is about it the ripping of the veil of the sky to reveal the engines of
       the machinery of Being.

ix

When poetry touches your heart, you realise that until that very moment
       you scarcely had one.
There is compassion in the deep well of it.
For no stone is left unturned by the detectives on its trail.
Poetry goes where man himself may not.
We may not cross the boundary of the living and the dead with impunity –
       but poetry can, because T.S. Eliot told us so, with this proviso:
'the communication / Of the dead is tongued with fire beyond the language
       of the living.'

x

The tongues of fire flicker on the Irish grass.
This is a green that hurts the eyes.
What we get is more than what we can see.
For the unravelling nature of Being is burgeoning in the fields, the
       floodgates of seeing are assaulted,
And that which is impossible is slowly taking place.
This is the *viriditas* of God, the green of the wild ecologist, the eco-warrior
       theological love.
Poetry is born in the fields of superabundance.
Men and women fall in love in its seismic embrace.
The ground is not safe when poetry rumbles.
All is the path perilous and nothing is the archer turning into Apollo.

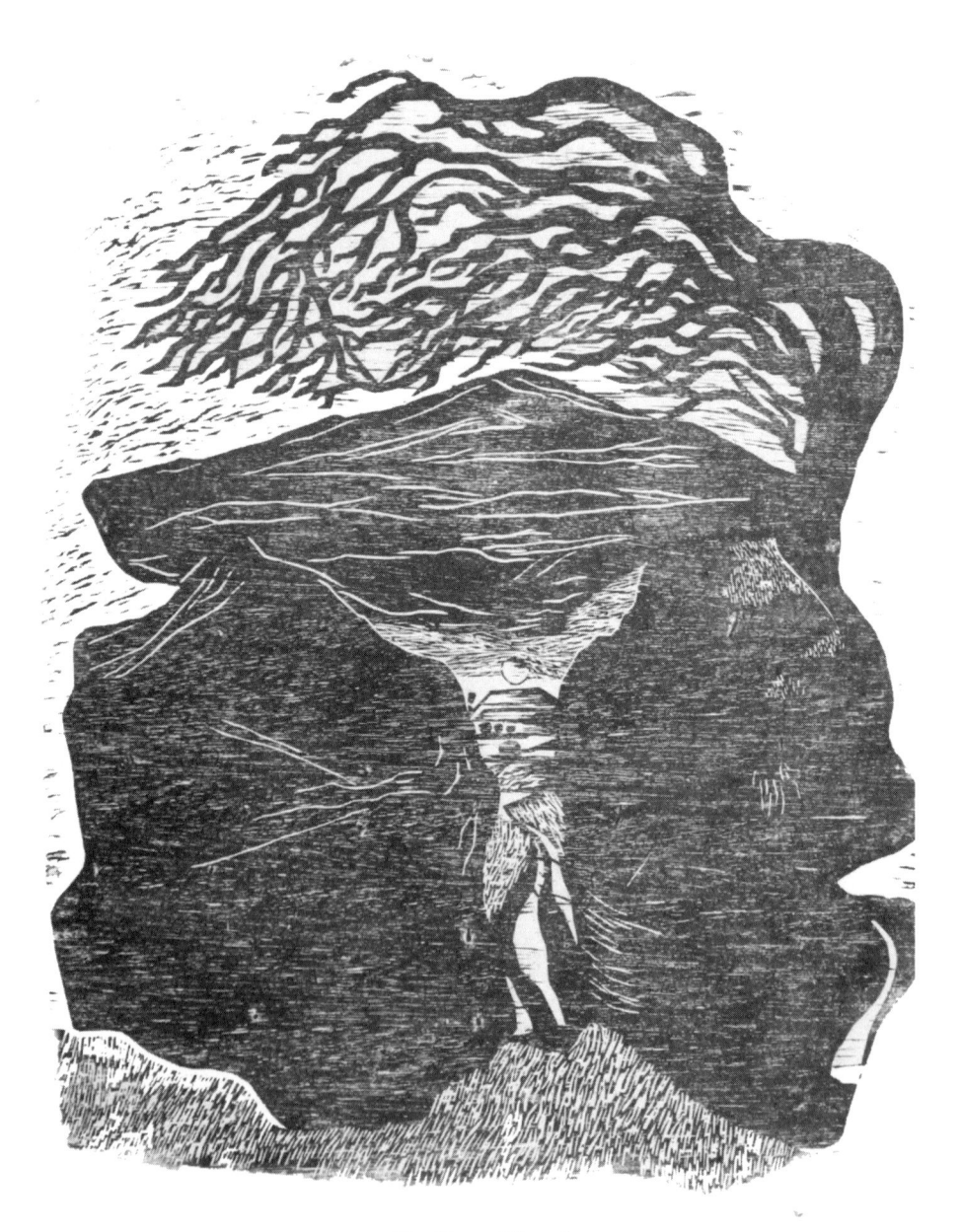

The Green Chapel

Biographies

Timothy Adès is a rhyming translator-poet, from French, Spanish, and German. His books to date are: *How to be a Grandfather* by Victor Hugo, and *33 Sonnets of the Resistance* and *The Madness of Amadis* by Jean Cassou. *Amadis* is from Agenda Editions. In prospect are two books of Robert Desnos: a big selection from Arc and the *Storysongs/Chantefables* from Agenda, both in bilingual text.

Thomas Adès, the son of Timothy Adès, was born in 1971 in London. He studied piano, composition and percussion at the Guildhall School of Music & Drama, and read music at King's College, Cambridge. He has composed many orchestral works. His first opera, *Powder Her Face*. was commissioned by Almeida Opera for the Cheltenham Festival in 1995, and his second opera, *The Tempest*, was commissioned by London's Royal Opera House. It premièred there in 2004 and was revived in 2007.

Karen Anderson is Publications Manager at Glyndebourne.

R.V. Bailey has published *Course Work* (Culverhay Press, 1997), *Marking Time* (Peterloo Poets, 2004), and *The Losing Game* (Mariscat Press 2010).For most of her life an academic, she was the extra voice in U. A. Fanthorpe's poetry readings; together they gave readings throughout the UK and overseas, jointly led poetry courses, and judged a range of poetry competitions. RVB regularly reviews poetry in *Envoi* and other magazines.

Sebastian Barker, born in Gloucestershire in 1945, was elected a Fellow of the Royal Society of Literature in 1997. He was also elected Chairman of the Poetry Society 1988-1992 and Editor of *The London Magazine* 2002-2008. He has been a Hawthornden Fellow; and a Royal Literary Fund Fellow at the University of Middlesex 2009-2011. He has represented the UK at international poetry festivals in Malaysia, Greece, and Lithuania. Sebastian is the author of fourteen books, twelve of them poetry. Subsequent publications include *Rowan Williams' Theology of Art & Other Essays* (Edwin Mellen 2010) and *A Theology of Poetry: The Wheels of Ezekiel* (Edwin Mellen 2010). Two new poetry collections have just been launched.

William Bedford is an award-winning novelist, children's novelist, poet and short-story writer, his work appearing in *Agenda, Critical Quarterly, Encounter, The Daily Telegraph, Essays in Criticism, The Independent Magazine, London Magazine, London Review of Books, The Nation, Poetry Review, The Southern Review, The Tablet, The Washington Times* and many others around the world. He is on the Editorial Board of *Poetry Salzburg Review*. His novel *Happiland* was shortlisted for the *Guardian* Fiction Prize. His selected poems, *Collecting Bottle Tops*, and selected short stories and non-fiction, *None of the Cadillacs Was Pink*, were both published in 2009. A new collection of poems, *The Fen Dancing*, is due to be published in March 2014.

Martin Bennett lives in Rome where he teaches and proofreads at the University of tor Vergata. He was this year's winner of the John Clare Poetry Prize.

Norman Buller was educated at Fircroft College, Birmingham and St. Catharine's College, Cambridge where he graduated in English. His verse has appeared widely in the U.K. and abroad and he has had four poetry collections – *Travelling Light* (2005), *Sleeping with Icons* (2007), *Fools and Mirrors* (2009) and *Powder on the Wind* (2011) – all published by Waterloo Press. His website is www.normanbuller.me.uk

Jane Clarke is originally from a farm in the west of Ireland and now lives in Wicklow. Her work is widely published in the UK and Ireland, including two poems in the Seren anthology, *Tokens for the Foundlings*. Her awards include Listowel Writers Week (2007), the iYeats (2010) and Poems for Patience (2013) www.janeclarkepoetry.ie

Joey Connolly is the editor of *Kaffeeklatsch*, a journal of poetry and criticism. His poetry has appeared in magazines including *PN Review, Magma, Stand*, and *Rialto*; he also reviews regularly for *PN Review* and for *Poetry Review*. In 2012 received an Eric Gregory award.

John F. Deane was born on Achill Island in 1943. He founded *Poetry Ireland* and *The Poetry Ireland Review*, 1979; published several collections of poetry and some fiction; won the *O'Shaughnessy Award for Irish Poetry*, the *Marten Toonder Award* for Literature, *Golden Key award* from Serbia, *Laudomia Bonanni Prize* from L'Aquila, Italy. Shortlisted for both the T.S.Eliot prize and The Irish Times Poetry Now Award, he won residencies in Bavaria, Monaco and Paris. He is a member of Aosdána . His recent poetry collections: *Eye of the Hare* came from Carcanet in 2011. *Snow falling on Chestnut Hill: New & Selected Poems* was published by Carcanet in October 2012. His latest novel, *Where No Storms Come*, was published by Blackstaff in 2010. He is current editor of *Poetry Ireland Review*. His selected poems have been published in Slovak translation, in Bratislava, Slovakia, 2013.

Greg Delanty, was born in Cork City, Ireland, in 1958. He has received many awards, most recently a Guggenheim for poetry. His *Collected Poems 1986-2006* is out from the Oxford Poets series of Carcanet Press. His latest nook is *The Greek Anthology, Book XVII* from Carcanet Press.

Sally Festing's second chapbook is *Salaams* (Happenstance, 2009). Her most recent book on Travelling Fair People will be out this year, and she co-runs the Saltmarsh Poetry in Burnham Market.

John Greening has published more than a dozen collections including *Hunts, Poems 1979-2009* and *To the War Poets* from Oxford Poets (Carcanet, November 2013). He has published guides to Yeats, Ted Hughes, Hardy, Edward Thomas, First World War Poets and the Elizabethans and a recent *Poetry Masterclass*. A regular reviewer with the TLS and a judge for the Eric Gregory Awards, Greening has received the Bridport Prize, the TLS Centenary Prize and a Cholmondeley Award for his poetry. He is currently editing Edmund Blunden's *Undertones of War* for OUP.

David Harsent has published nine volumes of poetry. *Legion*, won the Forward Prize for best collection 2005; *Night* (2011) was triple-shortlisted in the UK and won the Griffin International Poetry Prize. *In Secret*, his English versions of poems by Yannis Ritsos, was published in November 2102 in the UK and in the USA in 2013. Harsent has collaborated with composers – most often with Harrison Birtwistle – on commissions that have been performed at the Royal Opera House, the Royal Albert Hall (Proms), the Concertgebouw, the Wales Millennium Centre, The Megaron (Athens), the South Bank Centre, the Aldeburgh Festival, the Salzburg Festival and Carnegie Hall. David Harsent is Professor of Creative Writing at the University of Roehampton.

Eleanor Hooker's debut collection of poems *The Shadow Owner's Companion* (Dedalus Press) was published in 2012. She has a BA (Hons 1st) from the Open University, an MA (Hons.) in Cultural History from the University of Northumbria, and an MPhil in Creative Writing (Distinction) from Trinity College, Dublin. She was selected for the *Poetry Ireland* Introductions Series in 2011. Her poetry has been published in journals in Ireland and the UK. She is a founding member, Vice-Chairperson and PRO for the Dromineer Literary Festival. She is a helm and Press Officer for the Lough Derg RNLI Lifeboat. She began her career as a nurse and midwife.

Nigel Jarrett is a freelance writer and music critic based in Wales. He is a winner of the Rhys Davies Award for short fiction. In 2011 Parthian published *Funderland*, his debut collection of stories, which was universally praised in the national Press and elsewhere and longlisted for the Edge Hill Prize. His essays and poetry are published widely.

Simon Jenner was educated at Leeds, then Cambridge, where he gained a PhD. Jenner's debut came with two bi-lingual volumes published in Germany, in 1996 and '97. His British debut collection, *About Bloody Time*, was published by Waterloo Press in 2006. He had a South East Arts Bursary in 1999, Royal Literary Fund grants in 2003 and 2006. He has been Director of Survivors' Poetry since 2003 and from 2008-10, a Royal Literary Fund Fellow, at the Universities of East London and Chichester. A volume extending the imaginative heteronyms of Fernando Pessoa was published by Perdika Press. *Wrong Evenings* was published in 2011. A further Waterloo volume is forthcoming in 2012. An *Agenda* Edition of poems about composers and music will appear 2013. His poetry and articles appear in *Agenda, Angel Exhaust, PN Review*.

Wasfi Kani was born in 1956 in London's East End where her parents lived after leaving India at Partition. She studied music at St. Hilda's College, Oxford. After ten years working in the City, she made music her full time career in 1993. In 1987 she founded the Pimlico Opera and in 1997 she created Grange Park Opera in Hampshire. She received an OBE for her work in prison in 2002, and an Honorary Doctorate of Music in 2007.

Daniel K. Lee is a New York-based writer whose work has been seen in various online and print publications, including the recently published anothology *Between: New Gay Poetry*, and the forthcoming issues of *and/or* and *Berkeley Poetry Review*. He is sex and relationship advice writer at EmandLo.com and blog on culture and politics at danielextra.net. He holds a MFA in Creative Writing from the New School.

Sally Long is a postgraduate student of creative writing at the University of East London and has had poems published in print and online magazines including *Ink, Sweat and Tears, Snakeskin* and *South*. When not writing poetry she works as a teacher.

John Robert Lee (b. 1948), St. Lucian writer, has published several collections of poetry. His short stories and poems appear in international anthologies including the latest *The Oxford Book of Caribbean Verse (2005)*. His work is featured in *World Poetry Portfolio #58* edited by Sudeep Sen for Molossus (2013). Lee's latest collection of poetry is: *Sighting and other poems of faith* (2013), *elemental: new and selected poems* (Peepal Tree Press, 2008). In 2006, he co-edited with Saint Lucian poet and playwright Kendel Hippolyte, *Saint Lucian Literature and Theatre: an anthology of reviews*. He is the compiler of *Bibliography of St. Lucian creative writing 1948-2013* (2013). He writes an occasional blog at www.mahanaimnotes.blogspot.com.

Dan MacIsaac's poetry appeared in print most recently in *Vallum*, *CV2* and the Celtic Mists issue of *Agenda*. His poetry can also be viewed online, including at this.org and www.contemporaryverse2.ca. His verse translations have been published in a wide variety of journals.

Jim Maguire studied Music and English at University College Dublin. His work has appeared in *London Magazine*, *Stand* and *Poetry Ireland Review* among others and has received several prizes, including the Brendan Kennelly Award and the Strokestown International Poetry Prize. For many years he lived in Korea, the setting for his collection of short stories *Quiet People*. His first poetry collection, *Music Field*, was recently published by Poetry Salzburg.

Ann Joyce Mannion lives in Co. Sligo. Her poetry collection *Watching for Signs* was published by Dedalus Press. *Meadbh – The Crimson Path*, a CD of poetry, music and song in collaboration with composer and musician John Carty was released 2011. One of her poems, set to music by Crazy Dog Audio Theatre is included in the *Bee-Loud Glade* anthology published by Dedalus Press in 2011.

Giambattista Marino, 1569-1625, was born and died at Naples, but lived for long in Rome, Turin and Paris, where he was 'le Chevalier Marin'. His baroque style was greatly admired and much imitated. His epic work 'Adone' is the longest Italian poem.

Michael McCarthy is co-founder and Joint Artistic Director of *Music Theatre Wales*. From 1998-2012 he was Artistic Director of the contemporary opera studio for Norway. From 2007-2012 he was Dramaturg for Scottish Opera, and in 2012 he also led the Opera Creation Academy at the Festival d'Aix-en-Provence. Michael has staged over 40 contemporary operas and worked on more than 100 new works. Other productions include *Nabucco, La Traviata, Cosi fan Tutte* and *Don Giovanni*. Future projects include productions for Music Theatre Wales and *Tosca* in Norway.

Andrew McCulloch is a retired teacher of English and Education for the University of Huddersfield. His critical essays, reviews and poetry have appeared in *The English Review, PN Review* and the *TLS*.

Christine McNeill has published three poetry collections: *Kissing the Night* (Bloodaxe), *The Outsider* (Shoestring Press), and the latest *The Scent Gallery* (Shoestring Press, 2011). She has translated Rilke's poem-cycle *The Life of the Virgin Mary* (Dedalus Press), and with Patricia McCarthy co-translated Rilke's *The Book of Hours* (Agenda Editions). She is a tutor of German and creative writing, and lives in North Norfolk.

Stuart Medland has written two collections of poems for children, composed whilst still a primary school teacher in Norfolk. Much of his writing is inspired by natural history and a forthcoming book, *Rings in the Shingle*, published by Brambleby Books, is a poetic celebration of Norfolk wildlife inspired by his own photographic encounters. *Ouzel on the Honister*, a collection of poems taken from his many visits to the Lake District over the years, is in preparation with Original Plus. Stuart is now a regular contributor to *Agenda* and his collection, *Last Man Standing*, is due soon from *Agenda* Editions.

Nancy Anne Miller was born in Bermuda and has a MLitt in Creative Writing from the University of Glasgow. Her poems have appeared in *Edinburgh Review, Stand, Mslexia, The Caribbean Writer, Journal of Caribbean Literatures, Postcolonial Text, The Dalhousie Review, The Fiddlehead, Hampden-Sydney Poetry Review* and *International Literary Quarterly* among others. She was a MacDowell Fellow in 2008 and organized *Ber-Mused* a poetry event for Bermuda's 400[th]Anniversary.She leads poetry workshops in Bermuda.

Tim Murdoch's poetry has appeared over the years in *Agenda*, and elsewhere. He is preparing a poetry collection for publication.

David Pollard was born under the bed in 1942 and has been furniture salesman, accountant, TEFL teacher and university lecturer. He got his three degrees from the University of Sussex and has since taught at the universities of Sussex, Essex and the Hebrew University of Jerusalem. He has published *The Poetry of Keats: Language and Experience* which was his doctoral thesis, *A KWIC Concordance to the Harvard Edition of Keats' Letters*, a novel, *Nietzsche's Footfalls*, and four volumes of poetry, *patricides, Risk of Skin* and *bedbound*. The last, *Self-Portraits*, is just out.

Neil Powell is the author of *Benjamin Britten: A Life for Music* (Hutchinson, 2013). His previous books include *Roy Fuller: Writer and Society* (Carcanet, 1995), *The Language of Jazz* (Carcanet, 1997), *George Crabbe: An English Life* (Pimlico, 2004) and *Amis & Son: Two Literary Generations* (Macmillan, 2008), as well as seven collections of poetry, the most recent of which is *Proof of Identity* (Carcanet, 2012). He lives in Orford, Suffolk.

Herinder Rai is a recently self-taught and newly published British poet and songwriter-lyricist living in London. She is strongly inspired by the Romantics. Drawn to the musicality of poetry, she prefers to convey her emotions through auditory effects and visual imagery. She has been published in *The Coffee House* and *The New Writer*.

Jay Ramsay is the author of 35 books of poetry, non-fiction, and classic Chinese translation including *Alchemy, Crucible of Love–the alchemy of passionate relationships, Tao Te Ching, I Ching–the shamanic oracle of change, The Poet in You* (his correspondence course, since 1990), *Kingdom of the Edge–Selected Poems 1980-1998, Out of Time–1998-2008, Anamnesis–the remembering of soul* (in residence at St. James', Piccadilly) and *Places of Truth* (2009/2012). He is also poetry editor of *Caduceus* magazine, and works in private practice as a UKCP accredited psychosynthesis psychotherapist and healer.

Jay Rogoff has published four books of poems: *The Art of Gravity* (2011), *The Long Fault* (2008), *How We Came to Stand on That Shore* (2003), and *The Cutoff* (1995). Louisiana State University Press will issue his new collection, *Venera*, in 2014. His work has appeared in *Poetry Review* and *Stand*, and both his poetry and criticism in such American journals as *The Georgia Review, Literary Imagination, The Southern Review*, and *The Hopkins Review*, where he serves as dance critic. He lives in Saratoga Springs, New York, and teaches at Skidmore College.

Omar Sabbagh is a widely published poet and critic. His three extant poetry collections are, *My Only Ever Oedipal Complaint* and *The Square Root of Beirut* (Cinnamon, 2010/2012); and *Waxed Mahogany* (Agenda Editions, 2012). His monograph, *From Sight Through to In-Sight: Time, Narrative and Subjectivity in Conrad and Ford,* is forthcoming with Rodopi in early 2014. For the academic years, 2011-13, he was Visiting Assistant Professor in English Literature and Creative Writing at the American University of Beirut (AUB).

Labor/Naxos has recently re-issued **Eric Salzman**'s *The Nude Paper Sermon* (Texts: Steven Wade & John Ashbery); *Civilization & Its Discontents* (Text & Music with Michael Sahl); *Wiretap* (4 short pieces: 'Helix', 'Queens Collage','Wiretap'" & "'Larynx Music'. *Jukebox in the Tavern of Love* (Text: Valeria Vasilevsky)/ *Basket Rondo*, a new work by Meredith Monk (both commissioned by Western Wind) will be released early 2014. *Introduction to 20th Century Music* by Eric Salzman is published by Prentice Hall and *The New Music Theater: Seeing the Voice, Hearing the Body* by Eric Salzman and Thomas Desi is published by Oxford University Press. For more information, listening excerpts and ordering information: www.laborrecords.com/lab7092.html or www.ericsalzman.com

Eva Salzman's work has been recorded on BBC and performed at Huddersfield Festival, King's Place, Buxton Festival, English National Opera Studio and in Oslo, Dusseldorf & Vienna. Libretti/Songs include: *Cassandra* (Composer: Eric Salzman)/Singer & Musician: Kristin Norderval; *Shawna and Ron's Half Moon* (Composers: Philip Cashian/Ian McQueen/A.L. Nicholson); *One Two & Closing Time* (Composer Gary Carpenter). Recordings include The NMC Songbook and *Secret Life of a Girl* & *Romance & Revolution* (Singer/Composer: Christine Tobin). Books include *Double Crossing: New & Selected Poems* (Bloodaxe) and, as co-editor, the acclaimed anthology *Women's Work: Modern Women Poets Writing in English* (Seren). She is Associate Tutor at Goldsmiths: University of London.

Armand Silvestre, 1837-1901, was a graduate of the École Polytechnique: an 'X'. He became an Inspector of Finances, a high official. His drama *Henry VIII* was set to music by Saint-Saëns and a sacred stage work was set by Gounod. He wrote five illustrated volumes on the nude in art.

James Simpson is a Jerwood/Arvon Award Winner and a prizewinner in the Thomas Hardy Society's James Gibson Memorial Poetry Competition. He has collaborated with the artist and printmaker Carolyn Trant on the artist's book, *Hunting the Wren* (Parvenu/Actaeon Press) which was purchased by the British Library, Special Collections. Recently they have worked together on *The Untenanted Room* (Agenda Editions). His work has appeared in *Resurgence, Agenda, The Hardy Society Journal,* and *The London Magazine* and has been anthologised in *Our Common Ground* (Silverdart Publishing), a collection of poems celebrating farming and the countryside.

Robert Smith was born in London but now lives and works in Cambridge. He favours short forms, seeking for concentrated intensity of expression and sharp imagery. His work has previously been published in *Agenda*.

Warren Stutely is a retired bookseller and lives near the Thames in Teddington.

Jonathan Taylor is author of the novel *Entertaining Strangers* (Salt, October 2012), and the memoir *Take Me Home* (Granta Books, 2007). His poetry collection, provisionally entitled *Musicolepsy*, will be published by Shoestring Press in early 2013, and his collection of short stories, *Kontakte and Other Stories*, by Roman Books in late 2013. He is editor of *Overheard: Stories to Read Aloud* (Salt, 2012). He is Senior Lecturer in Creative Writing at De Montfort University, and co-director of arts organisation and small publisher, Crystal Clear Creators (www.crystalclearcreators.org.uk).

N. S. Thompson works as a translator. Recent poetry in *Able Muse* (USA), *New Walk, The Spectator* and *Stand*. Selections from his most recent book *Letter to Auden* (Smokestack, 2010) were first published in *Agenda*. Currently working on creating a poetry performance with synthesizer and sound effects, but hopes to find a composer to work on the *Ceyx and Alcyone* libretto.

Derek Walcott, poet, playwright and lecturer was born in 1930 in Castries, Saint Lucia. In 1992 he received the Nobel Prize for Literature. He has won many other awards and prizes for his poetry, including the 2011 T S Eliot Prize, for his poetry collection, *White Egrets*.

Sarah Wardle won *Poetry Review*'s new poet of the year award in 1999. Her first book, *Fields Away* (Bloodaxe, 2003) was shortlisted for the Forward best first collection prize. Her other books are *Score!* (Bloodaxe, 2005) and *A Knowable World* (Bloodaxe, 2009). She teaches at Morley College.

Laurelyn Whitt's poems appear in numerous, primarily North American, journals, such as *Nimrod International, PRISM International, Malahat Review, Tampa Review, Descant* and *Rattle*. The author of three award-winning poetry collections, including *Interstices* (Logan House Press), her new book, *Tether*, is forthcoming in 2013 from Seraphim Editions (Woodstock, Ontario). She lives in Minnedosa, Manitoba.

Susan Wick's most recent collection, *House of Tongues* (Bloodaxe, 2011), was a Poetry Book Society Recommendation. Her novel, *A Place to Stop*, came out from Salt in 2012 and was a *White Review* Reading Group choice. A second book of her translations of the French poet Valerie Rouzeau, *Talking Vrouz* (Arc, 2014), is the PBS Winter 2013-14 Recommended Translation.

Lawrence Wilson grew up near Chicago, Illinois, reversing his great-grandparents' century-old journeys when he emigrated to Britain in 2005. His poetry, essays, short fiction and reviews have appeared in publications such as *Albedo One, Poet's Cove, The Art of Monhegan Island,* and *Art and Academe,* and online at Salon, Amazon and monhegan.com. He has a BFA in theatre, an MA in education and an MFA in art, and is currently Head of English and Drama at Rose Hill, one of the oldest prep schools in England.

TEAR–OFF SUBSCRIPTION FORM

Pay by cheque (payable to 'Agenda'), or
Visa / MasterCard

SUBSCRIPTION RATES ON INSIDE FRONT COVER

1 Subscription (1 year) =

> 2 double issues
> 1 double, 2 single issues
> or
> 4 single issues
> (The above is variable)

Please print

Name: ....

Address: ....

....

....

.... Postcode ....

Tel: ....

Email: ....

Visa / MasterCard No: ☐☐☐☐ – ☐☐☐☐ – ☐☐☐☐ – ☐☐☐☐

Expiry date: ☐☐ – ☐☐

Please tick box:

    New Subscription ☐   Renewed Subscription ☐
    (or subscribe online – www.agendapoetry.co.uk)

Send to: AGENDA, The Wheelwrights, Fletching Street, Mayfield,
East Sussex, TN20 6TL
Tel: 01435-873703

Web supplement to
Poetry & Opera issue

Libretti:

Home: a libretto in search of a composer by **John Greening**

Ceyx & Alcyone: a libretto for an opera in two acts by **N.S. Thompson**

At your Feet: five settings of text by Kim Moore, chosen young Broadsheet poet, for Soprano and Piano – music by **Steven Jackson**

Essays:

Kim Moore: My Collaboration with **Steven Jackson**

James Aichison: Poetry and Music

Poems, artwork, including opera sketches by **Johnny Marsh**.

Broadsheets for young poets and artists

Visit the website also for news of Agenda workshops.

www.agendapoetry.co.uk

Alison Stump

Johnny Marsh

SUBSCRIBE FOR A FRIEND
ONLINE IF YOU WISH